Communication Studies:
An Introduction

Sheila Steinberg

ISBN 0 7021 5093 2

Book design and DTP: Charlene Bate, Cape Town
Cover design: Linda Lurie
Printed in South Africa by Creda Communications, Eliot Avenue, Eppindust, Cape Town

Contents

UNIT 2   NONVERBAL COMMUNICATION   43

UNIT 3   INTRAPERSONAL COMMUNICATION   67

UNIT 4   INTERPERSONAL COMMUNICATION   93

UNIT 7   MASS COMMUNICATION   169

List of figures

Foreword

In the past two decades or so, we have seen a proliferation of publications in communication science. However, it is still difficult to find a text book that provides a sound academic foundation in communication theory for first year students. The main problem is that the majority of books usually emphasise one or two fields of communication science, such as mass communication or organisational communication theory. The student is still not led to understand the media, interpersonal, group, organisational and other branches of communication theory within the context of the relationship between the different branches of theory. Furthermore, the majority of books are localised in terms of their examples, case studies and communication issues – usually they are British or North American. Although these books may contain good examples and case studies, it becomes a mammoth task for the lecturer and the student to replace them with local ones in order to conceptualise the theory against their own backgrounds and experiences. This problem is intensified in the case of distance education, which confronts the lecturer with distinctive didactic requirements.

In this text book, Sheila Steinberg addresses the problems outlined above. With a clear explanation of basic concepts and good examples, she leads the student through seven study units to an understanding of the foundations of communication study and the most prominent theories underlying nonverbal, intrapersonal, inter-personal, small-group, organisational and mass communication. Against the background of the Department of Communication of the University of South Africa's (Unisa) distance education requisites, she provides numerous study activities. These activities, as well as study skills and self-assessment tests (see the wrap-around study guide provided by Unisa Press) are in accordance with neatly worked-out and clear knowledge, skill and attitude outcomes set for each study unit.

I am convinced that this book, written by one of South Africa's senior scholars in communication science, will immensely benefit not only the first year level students it was written for, but will also be of great help to all communication lecturers and teachers. It sets the discipline in an African context and it sets the tone for a number of new outcomes-based books planned by Unisa's Department of Communication as a follow-up to its Course Book Series in Communication Studies, also published by Juta.

Professor Pieter J Fourie
Head of the Department of Communication
University of South Africa
Pretoria
August 1999

Foundations of communication study

Overview

The study of human communication is over two thousand years old. In the fourth century BC, for example, the ancient Chinese philosopher, Confucius, and the classical Greek philosopher, Aristotle, were both formulating ideas about communication. The study of communication is of particular interest today because of rapid developments in new technologies for producing and transmitting (sending) information. But communication scholars agree that, despite the proliferation of communication technologies, the human communication problems we have today are not basically different from those that people experienced hundreds of years ago. The consensus of opinion is that we are not going to solve communication problems by teaching people to master technology, but rather by helping them to gain insight into the phenomenon of communication (Trenholm 1991). One way of understanding communication is to study it scientifically in order to come closer to answering the question: what is communication?

scientific study
a disciplined and systematic approach to study

Unit 1 provides the foundation on which the *scientific study* of communication is based. We begin the unit by discussing the complex nature of communication. We first consider three definitions of communication and then gain further insight by examining the following dimensions of communication: verbal and nonverbal communication, oral and written communication, formal and informal communication, and intentional and unintentional communication. In the next part of the unit we explain the components that comprise the process of communication. We then discuss various models which illustrate different views of the communication process. We continue the unit with a brief description of the different contexts in which communication is studied today: intrapersonal communication, inter-personal communication, small-group communication, organisational communication, public speaking and mass communication. We conclude the unit with a case study which illustrates the process of communication in an organisational setting.

Learning outcomes

Our primary aim in this introductory text is to motivate you to learn about communication and to become actively involved in developing your communication competence. What do we want you to be able to do by the time you reach the end of this book? Firstly, we want you to obtain theoretical knowledge and understanding of communication. Secondly, we want you to think about what you have learned and relate your new knowledge to your own everyday experiences of communication. Thirdly, we want you to demonstrate your competence, for example by improving your relationships with other people. Fourthly, we want to encourage you to think critically about the material you study in this module, as well as any other information you come across during your studies. In each of the seven units that comprise this text, we have designed a list of learning outcomes to help you to achieve these aims.

At the end of this unit you should be able to do the following.

1   Define *communication* in three ways and explain how each definition provides a different view of the concept, using examples from your own experience of communication.

2   Explain how the dimensions of communication contribute to its complex nature.

3   Define and explain each of the components that comprise the process of communication, using examples from your own experience of communication.

4   Describe the various models in this unit, explaining the differences between them.

5 Define six contexts in which communication takes place. Explain the basis on which we differentiate between the contexts, illustrating your answers with examples from your own experience of communication.

6 Apply the principles you have learned in this unit to everyday experiences of communication.

7 Answer the questions based on the case at the end of this unit.

Introduction

We would probably all agree that we know what communication is and that we can recognise it when we see it. However, few words are used in as many different ways by as many different people. Some people immediately think about a conversation between friends, a politician making a persuasive speech, a minister delivering a sermon, or even the exchange of glances between lovers. Others immediately associate communication with mass media such as newspapers, radio and television. To some, communication brings to mind computers, cellular phones and satellites. Communication is also used to describe traffic signals, morse code, the sign languages of the deaf, uniforms, flags and telephone calls. A child's cry, a mother's kiss, a facial expression, graffiti on the wall of a public restroom, even silence, are also referred to as *communication*. It is equally difficult to describe why we use communication. People communicate to establish relationships with others, to express feelings and opinions, to share experiences, to work together efficiently, to be entertained, and to persuade others to think as they do. What is very clear is that communication is used to describe many things. For this reason, it is difficult to arrive at an exact definition of communication.

1.1 Defining communication

definition
a short, precise explanation of a word

As a student of communication, you may already have turned to your favourite dictionary to find a clear **definition** of the term. The *Oxford English Dictionary*, for example, will provide you not with a single definition, but with twelve different meanings! Should you search further in different books on the subject, you would find that there is little agreement among communication scholars about a definition — nearly every book on communication offers its own definition. In a survey of the literature on communication, Dance and Larson (1976) found that there were 126 definitions and, since then, even more definitions have been formulated.

One of the reasons for the proliferation of definitions is that there is no single approach to the study of communication. Definitions differ according to the **theorist's** views about communication. In the scientific study of communication, there are two general and basic views about communication: a **technical view** and a **meaning-centred view**. Theorists who adopt a technical view are concerned with how accurately and efficiently messages can be transferred from one person to another along a channel such as a telephone wire or the airwaves that carry sound and pictures to radios and television sets. They attempt to identify ways of increasing the clarity and accuracy of the message and concentrate on improving the tools and techniques that promote efficient communication, such as clear telephone lines or faster computers. Communication is seen as a linear (one-way) sequence of events from Person A to Person B. From a **technical** point of view, communication can be defined very simply as *sending and receiving messages*, or *the transmission of messages from one person to another*. However, solving technical or engineering problems does not tell us much about the complexity of communication or the human aspect of communication.

A second and more complex view of communication is that, in addition to the transmission of messages, it involves their interpretation and **meaning**. This view considers communication as a human phenomenon and the central aspect of human existence. Our ability to communicate is what distinguishes us from other forms of life. Meaning-centred theorists concentrate on issues such as what motivates people to communicate in the first place, how they give meaning to each other's messages, what happens between them during communication, and how

theorist
someone who expresses an idea about an aspect of communication

technical definition

process/meaning-centred definition

they use language to create and exchange meaningful messages. The emphasis is on the **interaction** between the participants in communication. From this point of view, communication can be defined as a *dynamic process of exchanging meaningful messages.*

process
a series of actions
or events

Defining communication as a **process** brings us closer to an understanding of the complexity of communication. In contrast to the technical view, considering communication as a process means that it is not a fixed, static thing; rather, it is dynamic, never-ending and ever-changing. It does not have a beginning or an end, nor does it follow a fixed sequence of events.

The use of the term *process* also tells us that communication is characterised by continuous evolution and change. We change others and are changed by them when we communicate. All the communication encounters you have had in the past, as well as all the information, ideas and opinions you have gathered, gradually change you and your behaviour, and consequently the way you communicate with others. According to Dimbleby and Burton (1985:31), "everything that we learn, every bit of information that we acquire changes our behaviour to some extent in the end. Every piece of communication which we experience may affect our attitudes and beliefs in some small way."

A process is also irreversible, which means that each communication encounter you have influences the one that follows. How you communicated with someone in the past can help or hinder your communication with them in the future. Should you have an argument with your partner before going to work, for example, your feelings may cause you to lash out at a colleague who asks an innocent question. The problem is that the next day, you and your colleague are unable to communicate as comfortably as before. Your reaction to the argument of the previous day has had an effect on your future communication with your colleague (Barker & Gaut 1996).

transactional definition

An extension of the process definition is the **transactional definition** of communication. Contemporary theorists regard communication not only as an interactive process of exchanging meaningful messages, but as a ***transaction*** between the participants during which a relationship develops between them. A transactional process is one in which the people communicating are mutually responsible for the outcome of the communication encounter as they transmit information, create meaning and elicit responses. The focus is on the **quality of the relationship** that develops between them, as well as on the transfer and interpretation of messages. Communication becomes a reciprocal process in which meaning is negotiated through the exchange of messages. From this perspective, communication is defined as a *transactional process of exchanging messages and negotiating meaning to establish and maintain relationships* (Verderber 1990). We prefer this definition because the concept of transaction suggests that the participants must arrive at some mutual agreement about the meaning of their messages for communication to be effective and for their relationship to be satisfying.

1.2 Dimensions of communication

The definitions we have discussed so far make it clear that the communication process is more complex than one person sending a message to another person. Considering questions such as the following brings us closer to an understanding of the nature of communication: are we communicating when we do not use words? To what extent is communication intentional? In the next section, we gain further insight into the complexity of communication by examining the dimensions of verbal and nonverbal communication, oral and written communication, formal and informal communication, and intentional and unintentional communication. The discussion is based largely on Barker and Gaut (1996).

1.2.1 Verbal and nonverbal communication

When we think of communication, we tend to think about spoken messages. But the way in which we understand messages depends on more than words. The tone of voice, gestures, use of space and touch, facial expressions, accent and dress of the communicator all influence our understanding. For example, when we give someone directions, we often point and use other gestures to clarify our spoken instructions. Communication scholars divide the 'language' of communication into two primary categories: verbal and nonverbal communication.

verbal communication

Verbal communication refers to the spoken or written signs called words which make up a particular language such as English or Zulu. People who speak the same language understand one another because they usually ascribe similar meanings to words. **Nonverbal communication** refers to all human communication that does not use written or spoken signs, such as a smile or a nod of the head. Although nonverbal signs have socially shared meanings, such meanings are not always universal. In traditional African society, for example, it is generally considered rude for someone to be higher than a person he or she respects. While a teacher entering the room in a Western school would expect the class to rise and greet her, most African pupils in rural schools would remain seated and not speak until spoken to (Finlayson 1991:9). When we study communication, we cannot separate the two categories because our clothing or tone of voice, for example, communicate a message even as we speak. Verbal and nonverbal signs thus work together to convey the meaning of a message. We discuss nonverbal communication in more detail in unit 2.

nonverbal communication

1.2.2 Oral and written communication

Oral and written communication both involve the use of words. **Oral communication** refers to messages that are transmitted aloud. We constantly participate in oral communication in our daily lives by speaking and listening. We may have a conversation with friends, watch a programme on television, listen to some music on the radio, attend a lecture, or telephone a classmate. From these examples, we can conclude that oral messages generally involve both verbal and nonverbal communication.

oral communication

written communication

Written communication is taking place right now as you read this book. Although this type of communication involves mainly words, it also has a nonverbal dimension. A handwritten birthday message, for example, usually evokes a different response than a printed card that was bought in a store — it communicates a somewhat more personal message. The graphics or diagrams that accompany the words in this book also communicate information nonverbally. Oral and written communication are sometimes used together. Many advertisements use graphics to make the oral message clearer. You may have seen an advertisement for toothpaste, for example, that uses graphics to reinforce the oral message that plaque causes damage to our gums if we do not brush our teeth regularly. Although oral and written messages differ in a number of ways, what is important is that they both involve the creation and sending of messages.

Figure 1.1: Graphics and words in an advertisement

1.2.3   Formal and informal communication

Two speakers debating an issue at a political gathering, the newsreader on television, a group of students chatting on campus, or some children playing games together, are all involved in communication. Whether we communicate formally or informally depends largely on the situation in which we find ourselves. When we are involved in *formal communication*, such as a job interview, we pay more attention to both our verbal and nonverbal messages. For instance, we tend to avoid using slang in our conversation, try to express ourselves clearly when answering questions, and pay particular attention to grammar. We are also more concerned about the image that our nonverbal communication conveys. For example, we would dress carefully for a job interview, make sure that our hair is neat, and consciously sit up straight to create the desired impression.

formal communication

When we are involved in *informal communication*, such as talking to friends at a party, we are more at ease and can communicate more naturally. You are probably aware from your own experience that, when you communicate informally, your verbal messages are less structured and you pay less attention to nonverbal messages such as clothing and posture. While you might feel that you are being yourself by sitting on the floor at a friend's house, for example, it is unlikely that you would do so in your boss's office — you would not be communicating the desired image.

informal communication

1.2.4   Intentional and unintentional communication

All communication has a purpose — we communicate for a reason. However, we are not always aware that we have communicated a message. *Intentional communication* occurs when we communicate with a specific goal in mind. For example, at your graduation ceremony, you intentionally thank your parents for all the help and support they have given you over the years. You reinforce your message nonverbally with a smile and a hug. Or, you engage in conversation with someone at a party because you want to come across as friendly. You also know that

intentional communication

FOUNDATIONS OF COMMUNICATION STUDY   **9**

the speaker at a wedding, for instance, deliberately includes several jokes in his speech to get the guests to relax and enjoy themselves. You turn on the radio with the intention of catching up on the latest news. However, there are times when we communicate messages we never intended.

unintentional communication

Unintentional communication refers to the occasions when communication takes place without the communicator being aware of it. A friend might tell you that he is not upset by the fact that you forgot to call on his birthday, but the look on his face tells another story. While our verbal communication is almost always intentional, our unintentional messages are usually nonverbal. The way that people use gestures, tone of voice and other nonverbal signs often speaks louder than words. Then there is another type of unintentional communication. Consider the following example: a young man whistling cheerfully passes you on the street. You think to yourself, 'he's in a good mood today'. The young man, of course, is totally unaware that he has communicated a message to you, a complete stranger. The point to remember is that communication has occurred, whether it was intended or not.

1.3 Components of the communication process

The definitions and dimensions we have discussed thus far have probably given you the impression that communication is not an easy topic to study. One way to understand the communication process is to study it as a system. A ***system*** is any entity that is composed of interdependent parts working together to achieve an intended goal. An example of a system is the human body. The individual parts such as the heart, lungs, liver, kidneys, and so on, all work together to keep the body functioning efficiently. Should something happen to prevent the lungs, for example, from obtaining oxygen, it is not only the lungs that are affected. The heart is put under strain and this in turn affects the blood supply to all the other organs. We can study communication in much the same way by identifying its ***components*** or ***elements*** and analysing how the components affect one another during the communication process. We should then have a better idea

system

components/ elements parts of the communication process

of 'what happens' when we communicate and perhaps be able to improve our communication knowledge and skills.

We use communication terms or concepts to identify and explain the components of the process. The definitions we give to the components in the communication process turn them into concepts. A **concept** is a word to which all scientists in a field of study (such as psychology, law, medicine, communication) attach the same meaning so as to enable them to understand one another. We always formulate our thoughts in concepts. We cannot think of an object (a motor car), an event (a funeral), or a person (a well-known political leader) without forming a mental image or concept of the object, event or person. In scientific study scientists deliberately try to avoid confusion by consistently using concepts with the same meanings. Later on we will see that concepts are indispensable for describing communication models.

concept
a word with a specific meaning in communication

Figure 1.2: The communication process

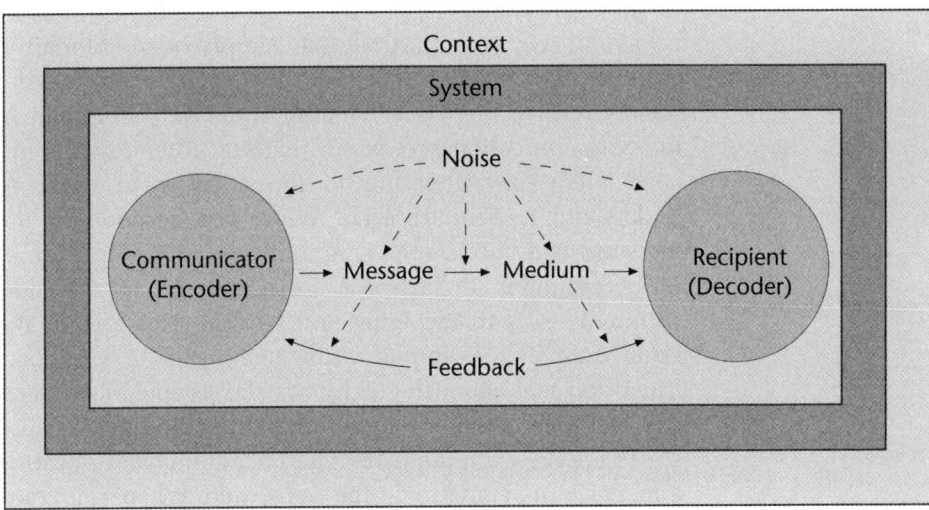

(Adapted from Barker & Gaut 1996)

Figure 1.2 gives us a visual representation of the communication process. Take note that, although we discuss the components separately for the purpose of analysis, they are not isolated entities, but occur almost simultaneously as the process evolves. The discussion that follows is based mainly on Verderber (1990); Hybels and Weaver (1995); and Barker and Gaut (1996).

1.3.1 People

The people involved in the communication process are usually referred to as the message source and the message receiver. However, source and receiver sound like technical terms, and as we are discussing human communication, we prefer to call them *communicator* and *recipient*. Because communication is a dynamic process, people are never exclusively communicators or recipients; each participant in the interaction plays both roles.

communicator

recipient

As a **communicator**, you intentionally form purposeful messages and attempt to express them to others through verbal and nonverbal signs. You usually use both words and gestures to put your message across. Your purpose may be the need to share your thoughts and feelings, or perhaps to persuade someone to change an attitude, opinion or behaviour. Or, your purpose may simply be to entertain a group of friends by telling a joke. As a **recipient**, you do not merely receive messages. You are an active participant in the communication process in that you intentionally and consciously pay attention to the message in order to understand and interpret it. When you respond to the message, you become the communicator and your partner is the recipient. In fact, you are usually 'communicator-recipient' — both receiving and sending messages at the same time. For example, while you listen to your best friend tell you about the bad news she received last night, you may instinctively put out a hand to touch her because she is upset — you are listening to her and communicating a message of sympathy at the same time. When you come across the terms *communicator* and *recipient* (or sender and receiver), remember that they are used more as a convenience than as an accurate description of the roles of the participants in the communication process.

1.3.2 Message

message

Communication takes place through the sending and receiving of messages. The ***message*** has a content which is conveyed during the communication encounter. The content may be factual information or it may be the ideas, thoughts and feelings expressed by the participants. Some messages have a clear and obvious content, while others are hidden or not so obvious. For example, a friend might tell you overtly that she has not seen anyone for the past two weeks because she has been ill. Covertly, she could be telling you that she is lonely and wants your company. Messages thus have meaning which must be understood and interpreted. Because people cannot transfer meaning from one mind to another, they use signs and codes to formulate messages. It would not be possible to communicate your ideas and feelings if you did not have signs to represent them. Communication is all about sending and receiving signs which have meanings attached to them.

1.3.3 Sign and code

sign

verbal/ nonverbal signs

A ***sign*** is something that stands for something else — a particular thing or idea. Smoke is a sign of fire. The South African flag is a sign that represents or stands for South Africa. The words and diagrams in this book are also signs. ***Verbal signs*** are spoken and written words and sounds, whereas ***nonverbal signs*** are cues or signals that are transmitted without the use of sound. As you speak, you choose words or verbal signs to convey your meaning. But, as we discussed in section 1.2.1, your verbal message is accompanied and given additional meaning by nonverbal signs — your body movements, facial expressions, tone of voice and hand gestures. When you listen to others, the nonverbal signs they use affect the meaning you assign to the verbal signs. For example, a friend who says, 'Yes, I'm interested in what you are telling me', but flips through the pages of a magazine while you are talking, is actually conveying a different message.

There are problems associated with signs which make it difficult to always agree on what they mean. One such problem is that the same sign can have different meanings for different people. For example, we can differentiate between concrete and abstract signs. When we use the word *pencil*, we agree that we are talking about something which with we write. *Pencil* is a **concrete sign** which represents an object. **Abstract signs** stand for qualities, ideas or attributes. Words such as *love*, *clever* or *democracy* do not denote an actual object. You can see from these examples that concrete signs or words carry more specific meanings than abstract words. The meaning we ascribe to abstract words depends largely on our individual background and past experiences. Since people's background and experiences differ, they may not agree on the meaning of some words, and there is more likely to be a breakdown in communication between them. When we use signs to formulate messages, we cannot simply assume that the words we use have exactly the same meaning for others as they do for us.

concrete/ abstract signs

A second problem that creates misunderstandings is the fact that words have denotative and connotative meanings.

denotative meaning

The **denotative** meaning of a word is the explicit, literal meaning that is provided in a dictionary and which is accepted at a given time by all the people who use the word. But denotation is not always that simple. Most dictionaries, for example, provide more than one meaning for the same word. *Strike*, for instance, has at least three denotative meanings: workers go 'on strike' to negotiate better working conditions. But we also 'strike' a match or 'strike' up the band. In fact, you will find many more meanings for the word *strike* in a dictionary. To complicate matters, no two dictionaries will have the same meaning for abstract concepts such as *love* or *justice*. Moreover, words change in meaning over time. If you had described someone as *gay* in the 1960s, everyone would have understood that you meant happy or cheerful. Today, 'gay' is most often used as a synonym for 'homosexual'. So, if you describe someone as *gay* when you mean happy or cheerful, you run the risk of being totally misunderstood.

connotative meaning

The **connotative** meaning of a word generally cannot be found in a dictionary. Connotation refers to the emotions and evaluations that an individual associates with a word.

It is the personal or subjective interpretation which is attached to a word as a result of one's background and past experiences. In other words, our connotative meanings vary according to our feelings for the object or concept we are considering. Research has shown that gender, for example, influences connotative meanings. A study by Arnold and Libby (1970) investigated male and female responses to sex-related words in an attempt to identify differences in response. Not surprisingly, it was found that women tend to respond much less favourably than men to words such as wife swapping, husband swapping, whore and prostitute (Tubbs & Moss 1991).

While denotation may affect meaning, an awareness of connotative meanings is essential if we are to avoid misunderstandings in our communication encounters. We need to be aware, for instance, that a particular word may evoke a positive connotation in one person, but a negative connotation in another. Consider the word *communism*. According to a dictionary, its denotative meaning is a theory or system of social organisation based on holding common property. However, for some people the word *communism* has the negative connotation of revolutionary threat and upheaval, whereas for others the idea of common and shared property has a positive connotation.

code

Signs are combined in a systematic way according to codes. A *code* is a system for using signs. The system is based on rules or conventions shared by those who use the code. For example, speech is made up of a sequence of sound signs (words). But the act of speaking involves knowing which sign goes where (Dimbleby & Burton 1985). Grammar is the code for the use of speech. We combine words to form sentences according to the rules of the language we use. If we did not agree on these rules, we would not be able to communicate at all. The practice of using and combining certain signs becomes established over time as a social convention or fixed pattern in society. Bear in mind that language is not our only means of communication. We are also familiar with traffic signs or pictorial signs, for instance. We can regard such groups of signs or sign systems as 'languages', each made up of special types of signs with its own special code. For example, we know how to behave at the traffic lights because the traffic code in our society provides the rules by which we understand the combination of the colour signs red, green and amber. The traffic code is a social convention.

1.3.4 Encoding and decoding

encoding

Encoding is the process of taking the ideas in your mind and transforming them into verbal and nonverbal signs so that they can be transmitted as messages to someone else.

decoding

Decoding, on the other hand, is the process of taking the verbal and nonverbal messages that you receive from others and giving them meaning. In other words, we encode or create messages, and decode or give meaning to other people's messages. We are usually not aware of either the encoding or decoding process because we have been communicating since childhood. We do not consciously think about each word and gesture that we use. However, a teacher preparing a lesson may go through a conscious encoding process to select the best words to explain a difficult topic to her pupils. Likewise, should you choose to learn a foreign language, you would consciously be aware of both the encoding and decoding processes — such as the rules of grammar — until you become proficient in that language.

1.3.5 Medium and channel

After a message has been encoded by the communicator, it has to travel to the recipient. The medium and the channel are both links between the communicator and the recipient.

medium

The *medium* is the physical means by which messages are transmitted between people in communication. Your voice and body movements, as well as technological and electronic means of communication such as the telephone, a loudspeaker, newspapers, a book, a photograph, or the television set, are mediums (media) of communication. Think back to the dimensions of communication we discussed in section 1.2 and you will realise that different media have different requirements of which we as communicators must be aware. Whereas the physical appearance of a radio presenter will not influence the recipients of the message, the personal appearance of the speaker at a seminar could influence the way in which the audience (recipients) receives the message.

channel

The *channel* is the route by which the messages travel. The light waves that carry the television image or the airwaves that carry the sound of your voice are channels of communication, as are your five senses — hearing, sight, smell, touch and taste. We may **hear** a musical programme on the radio, **watch** a soccer match on television, **smell** fresh coffee as we walk down the street, **hug** a friend we have not seen for some time, or **taste** the flavours in a dish of curry. The channel has little to do with the meaning of the message and has become largely the concern of technical theorists (refer to section 1.1) whose interest in communication is to measure and maximise the capacity of a given channel to convey information (O'Sullivan, Hartley, Saunders & Fiske 1983).

1.3.6 Meaning

meaning

Meaning is an extremely difficult term to define because of its abstract nature. O'Sullivan et al (1983) suggest that, rather than try to define the term, we should regard meaning as the product or result of communication. In other words, the act of communication produces meaning. To enable us to better understand the concept, we could say that messages contain two types of information to which we attach meaning: content information and relational information. The **content level** refers to factual information about the topic of the message — what it is about. The **relational level** determines how the participants understand their relationship — it provides information about the feelings of the communicator and how the content should be interpreted. For instance, the message 'Let's discuss this problem' could be a request when a friend is talking to you, but a command when it is your boss who conveys the message. The content is the same, but the tone of voice and the way in which the message is delivered serve to define your relationship. Often, it is the relational level of a message rather than the content that tells you whether a

*content level/
relational level*

person is expressing affection or dislike, and whether or not a comment is humorous or sarcastic. We also need to be aware that meaning is not fixed. People are unpredictable and we cannot always be sure that they will react to a message in the way we intended.

1.3.7 Interpretation

interpretation

The meaning in a message must be interpreted. **Interpretation** involves more than a literal understanding of the signs in a message — it means that you add your own individual meaning to what is being conveyed. Interpretation depends on both social (shared) meanings and individual (personal or subjective) meanings. *Social* in this sense indicates that, to be able to begin communicating, we must have something in common. For example, we must share some basic understanding of verbal signs — we must speak the same language. We usually also share an understanding of what certain words mean in our culture, such as *democracy* or *justice*. But the way in which we use these words and what we understand by them is expressive of our personal and individual character (refer to the discussion of abstract words in section 1.3.3). Should you and I attend the same political meeting, for instance, we may well ascribe different meanings to the ideas expressed by the speaker because each of us is the product of our individual background, past experiences, sex, attitudes, feelings, ideas, values, occupation, religion and culture. For example, if you have been discriminated against in the past because you are a woman, or black, or a Moslem, the meaning that you assign to the word *justice* would differ from that of someone who has never experienced discrimination. The important point is that interpretation is never right or wrong. There may be different, but equally valid, interpretations for individual recipients of the same message.

1.3.8 Noise

Any stimulus that interferes with the transmission and reception of messages so that the meaning is not clearly understood creates a barrier between the communicator

noise

and the recipient. We call such barriers noise. **Noise** is more than distracting physical sounds, such as traffic noises or the yells of children that could make it difficult to hear the message. It is anything that interferes with the success of the communication by distorting the message so that the meaning received is different from that which is intended. The outcome of your encounter often depends on how you cope with external, internal and semantic noise.

external noises

External noises are stimuli in the environment that distract your attention. A bad odour, for instance, a cold room, an uncomfortable chair, the static on a telephone line, or even a pair of sunglasses can interfere with the transmission and reception of messages. You could be attending a lecture in a hot, overcrowded room and become so uncomfortable that you cannot concentrate on what the lecturer is saying. Blurred type or creased pages create noise in written communication because they interfere with the clarity of the communicator's message. Think about the following examples: do you hear the announcements at stations and airports clearly? If not, why not? What happens to the conversation when you communicate with someone who has a stutter or other speech impediment?

internal noises

Internal noises are the thoughts and feelings in people that may interfere with communication. Your moods, personal prejudices, as well as the amount of attention you pay to others, are all internal noises that influence the way you interpret messages. For instance, a student doesn't hear the lecture she is attending because she is thinking about the dance she is going to that evening. A man may be so resentful about having a woman appointed as his manager that he does not fully concentrate on what she is saying. If his bias (thoughts) prevents the accurate reception of her messages, then internal noise has occurred.

semantic noises

Semantic noises are interferences that occur when people have different meanings for words and when these meanings are not mutually understood. For example, if at the airport you ask your departing friend about his itinerary, and he replies that he hasn't packed one, then you know that he has not understood your message because he does not know what an itinerary is (Barker & Gaut 1996). Semantic noise also occurs when your doctor uses unfamiliar medical terms to explain why you are feeling ill. The result could be that you will be uncertain of what the problem is because he has created semantic noise by using words you do not understand. Similarly, other people may react in a way that you did not intend to your use of slang, ethnic slurs, foreign words, sexist remarks or profanity, thereby distorting the interaction between you. Semantic noise can also be caused by social and cultural differences between communicator and recipient because they may use different words to denote the same object or idea. One way of overcoming noise is by means of feedback.

1.3.9   Feedback

feedback

Feedback is the response of the participants to each other. During communication, the participants continuously send messages or feedback to each other. Feedback can be verbal or nonverbal. For instance, you tell me a joke and I smile. The smile is feedback. Or, I explain a problem to you and you ask for more information. The information I give you is also feedback. A shrug of the shoulders in response to a message is feedback, as is the applause of the audience to a speaker at a meeting. Feedback is important because it lets the participants know whether they have ascribed the same meaning to a message. In the examples of semantic noise described above, for example, feedback between the participants would have helped to clarify the misunderstandings.

interactive
a two-way process

linear process
moving in one direction

Feedback also gives communication its dynamic nature by making it an **interactive** rather than a **linear process**. Feedback is the means whereby we negotiate ideas and exchange meaning. Without feedback, it is not possible to discuss an issue or a feeling, exchange opinions or arrive at a mutually satisfactory conclusion to the communication encounter. It also allows people to monitor their performance by telling them how they are 'coming across'. A smile from your partner is positive feedback and encourages you to continue a conversation. Should you, however, receive negative feedback, such as a sarcastic remark, you may decide to terminate the conversation. It is therefore important to pay attention to the responses and reactions of others.

1.3.10 Context

context

Communication does not take place in a void. People always communicate within a situation or setting. ***Context*** refers to the environment, the place or conditions, in which the communication encounter takes place. A doctor's office is a context, as is the manager's office in an organisation. Communication is always contextual and is influenced by factors such as the time, place and physical properties of the meeting place, as well as the roles, status and relationships of the participants. People express themselves differently depending on, for instance, how well they know each other, whether they are at home or at work, and what their formal position is. While the school hall is a good place for giving speeches and presenting scholastic awards, it is not conducive to intimate conversations. In the same way, the school principal and a teacher will communicate more formally during working hours than when they meet socially at a party.

Putting all the components of the communication process or system together, we could say that a communicator encodes a message, using verbal and nonverbal signs and codes, which is carried by a medium along a channel to the recipient who decodes the message to understand it, interprets it to give it personal meaning, and responds via feedback. The presence of noise in any part of the system could affect the outcome of the encounter. Each component in the process influences and is influenced by every other component. Should your nonverbal behaviour, for example, create noise because the recipient perceives you as arrogant, she may decide to terminate the conversation by withholding feedback, and the relationship between you would not have a chance to develop.

1.4   Models of the communication process

One of the ways in which scholars have sought to understand the nature of communication is by means of *models*

models which describe and explain the communication process. We used a simple model in figure 1.2 to help you to visualise how the components in the communication process relate to one another. Models are visual diagrams of abstract ideas. The basic purpose of a model is to capture the essential features of a real situation in a simplified form so that it can be described, explained and understood more easily. In the same way that an architect's plan, for example, helps us to see what a house will look like upon completion, communication models help us to visualise the process of communication more clearly. Communication theorists use models to identify relevant components of the process and to provide a picture of how the components relate to each other during a real communication encounter. Models can be said to reflect the view of communication presented by a particular theorist.

A limitation of models is that they often provide simplified pictures of communication because they present only the aspect of the communication process a particular theorist wishes to emphasise. For example, one theorist may be interested in explaining how persuasion is used to change people's attitudes towards a social problem, while a second theorist may want to describe how a group of people reaches consensus about a problem that has arisen in the organisation where they work. In each case, certain aspects of the communication process will be emphasised and other aspects will be omitted. Despite the fact that they present a simplified view of communication, models are useful 'tools' in that they allow us to start thinking more critically about communication.

The models we have selected illustrate the different views of communication expressed in the definitions in section 1.1. We discuss the models in their historical context to enable you to gain a sense of the process by which scholars have come to understand the communication process over time. The discussion is based mainly on the succinct history of communication study provided by Ruben (1984). We begin with the writings of Plato and his pupil, Aristotle, who were central figures in the early study of rhetoric or persuasive speaking in classical Greece.

1.4.1   The classical view of communication

Communication as a field of academic study became established at universities in the Western world during the twentieth century. However, a systematic study of communication can be traced to the classical Greeks (between the fourth and fifth centuries BC). Their focus was on the study of *oratory* — the creation and delivery of spoken messages — which reflected the essentially oral nature of Greek society. Greek interest in understanding oratory grew out of the practical needs of day-to-day life. Greece had the first true democratic government in history — the people literally governed themselves. Business, government, education and law were conducted orally in public, and every Greek citizen had the right to participate in public affairs. For example, the Assembly (seat of government) was open to all free male citizens of adult age, regardless of income or class. It met about forty times a year and anyone present could speak about any topic — provided he could hold the audience's attention (Bowra 1966). The judicial system was similarly dependent upon oral communication. Greek citizens had to be their own lawyers and be able to present a case which would convince a jury of several hundred persons of their innocence. Effective public speaking or oratory, and the ability to use persuasive forms of communication therefore became a priority for the majority of people. Consequently, a group of teachers, called *sophists*, became popular by teaching people the art of *rhetoric* — how to prepare a persuasive speech and deliver it eloquently; in other words, how to become an effective orator.

Plato (427–347 BC) was sceptical of the professional sophists who earned a living by teaching orators to sway an audience. Plato maintained that the method used by the sophists — sophistic rhetoric — was not ethical because the orator was taught to persuade the audience unconditionally, even if this meant manipulating the emotions of the audience or presenting a one-sided argument which was aimed at deceiving the audience. Plato developed an alternative to the sophistic method — philosophical rhetoric — which was directed at persuading an audience by ethical

oratory
public speaking

sophist
professional teacher of rhetoric in ancient Greece

rhetoric
principles of creating and delivering a persuasive speech

FOUNDATIONS OF COMMUNICATION STUDY   **23**

means. Plato regarded each member of the audience as an individual and would present, for example, both sides of a discussion and give the listeners the opportunity to consider the argument in relation to their own needs and values. We could say that Plato gave the audience the opportunity to interpret the message within their own circumstances (refer to section 1.3.10). Plato's views, together with those of his pupil, Aristotle, contributed significantly to the body of knowledge about communication in classical times.

Like Plato, Aristotle (385–322 BC), regarded rhetoric as an art (or skill) that could be taught and as a field of academic study. Of the writings that survive from classical Greece, the most important is Aristotle's *Rhetoric* — a set of lecture notes on public speaking — which is still used as a reference work in departments of communication today. *Rhetoric* combines Aristotle's knowledge of communication with observations he made in everyday situations of the practices of speakers and the responses of audiences. Amongst other issues, Aristotle's *Rhetoric* contains his views about logic and truth in argumentation, various aspects of human nature, and the importance of the delivery of the speech, including the orator's style of speaking. Aristotle maintained that people could be taught (and should practise) the skilful construction of an argument and effective delivery of a speech.

Figure 1.3: Aristotle's view of communication

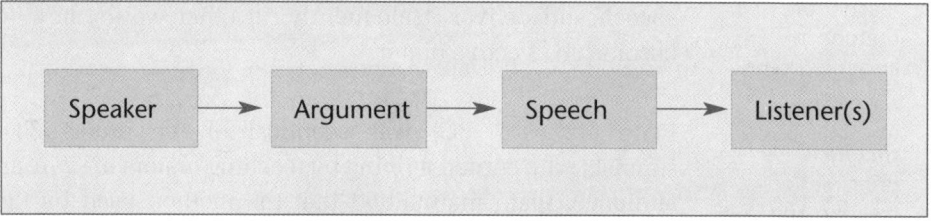

Aristotle described communication in terms of an orator or speaker constructing an argument to be presented in a speech to listeners — an audience. The speaker's goal was to present a positive image of himself and to make sure that members of the audience were receptive to the message. In Aristotle's words (translated by Roberts 1924:1377b):

rhetoric exists to affect the giving of decisions ... the orator must not only try to make the arguments of his speech demonstrative and worthy of belief; he must also make his own character look right and put his hearers, who are to decide, into the right frame of mind.

The ancient Romans also took public speaking very seriously and training in rhetoric and the correct use of language began at a young age. While the Greeks invented the science of rhetoric, Roman scholars such as Cicero (106–43BC) and Quintilian (35–95AD) broadened and perfected it. However, with the decline of the Classical period, democracy and the oral tradition began to wane. This can be attributed mainly to changes in society. For more than a thousand years after the fall of the Roman Empire, totalitarian regimes prevailed in Europe, and public opinion was no longer relevant in the political process. Deprived of the opportunity to sway masses of people through rhetoric, people no longer needed to be able to speak effectively, and academic interest in communication fell into insignificance. At the same time, the Church established complete control of religious practices, going so far as forbidding clergymen to preach. As a result, interest in rhetoric by religious scholars and other intellectuals also waned (Stacks, Hickson & Hill 1991).

medieval
Middle Ages (7th to 13th century AD)

There was a rebirth of learning during the late **Medieval** and **Renaissance** periods, and rhetoric was once again being studied in religion. However, it was not until a new society emerged as during the Industrial Revolution that the academic study of communication was revived.

Renaissance
revival of art, literature and learning in Europe in the 14th, 15th and 16th centuries

1.4.2 Twentieth-century views of communication

The Industrial Revolution, which began in Britain in the late eighteenth century and spread in the nineteenth century to Western Europe and the United States, created societies characterised by large-scale manufacturing industries rather than trade or farming. The invention of steam-powered machinery and the mass migration of people from rural areas to seek employment in the rapidly growing industrial cities brought about far-reaching changes in the nature of society. Although the printing press had been invented in the sixteenth century, it was only with the invention of the machinery that made the mass distribution of newspapers and other printed materials possible, that information became available to growing numbers of people. With the spread of printed materials, more and more people learned to read and write, and their thinking was freed from the restrictions of church and government. New political and religious ideas began to circulate in society, and throughout Europe and America revolutionary movements emerged, making use of print to disseminate their ideas to increasingly receptive publics. Particularly with the spread of newspapers, public opinion once again became something that political leaders had to take into account. Scholars began to revive the art of public speaking, and journalism developed into a field of study that contributed significantly to the body of knowledge about communication.

In the first half of the twentieth century, interest in communication continued in rhetoric and speech. The study of journalism was broadened by the advent of radio in the 1920s and television in the 1940s. As these media became firmly established in society, new areas of study emerged — mass media and mass communication. Investigations into the social impact of the mass media included questions such as: what effect does television violence have on children? At the same time, scholars from other disciplines began writing about the nature of communication and its role in human life. These disciplines included anthropology, sociology, psychology and languages, and their contributions also advanced the study of communication.

Communication was established as a field of study at universities in the late nineteenth century, but it was mainly housed in departments of English literature. In the early part of the twentieth century, individual communication departments began to emerge and, in the late 1940s, the first attempts at describing the nature of the communication process began to appear in the literature on communication. Some of the earliest views of communication were those of

Lasswell, Shannon and Weaver, and Schramm. The models they created reflect the development of communication from a linear to an interactive process (refer to section 1.1).

1.4.3 Lasswell's view of communication

Lasswell's model

Harold Lasswell was an American political scientist whose main interest was in the area of propaganda. In 1948, he described a view of communication that emphasises the effect of a message on the recipient(s). He said that the communication process could best be explained by asking the following questions: who? says what? to whom? in what channel? with what effect?

Figure 1.4: Lasswell's model of communication (after Lasswell 1948)

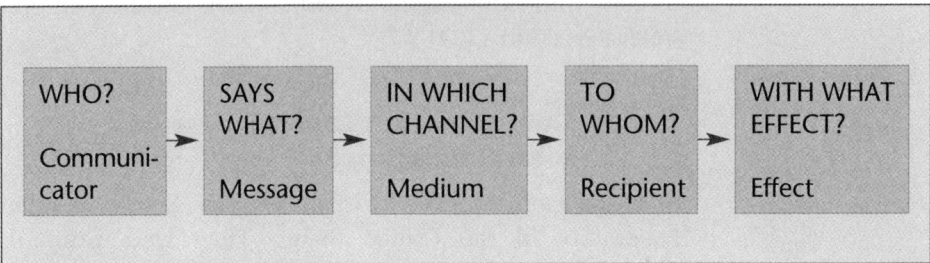

In the model, *who* refers to the communicator who formulates the message; *what* is the content of the message; *channel* indicates the medium of transmission; and *whom* describes either an individual recipient or the audience of mass communication. *Effect* is the outcome of the message which, for Lasswell, should be that the recipient will be persuaded to adopt a particular point of view. Note that the model focuses our attention on the individual components of the communication process and emphasises that the components occur in a sequence that begins with the communicator and ends with the recipient.

Lasswell's view of communication is similar to the way Aristotle depicted communication some two thousand years earlier (refer to figure 1.3). Ruben (1984) points out that both theorists focus primarily on verbal messages and emphasise the relationship between communicator, message and recipient. For both Lasswell and Aristotle, communication is a one-way process in which the communicator influences others through the content of the message. It therefore assumes that only the communicator is an active participant in the process, and that the recipient plays a passive role.

Because of technological developments that took place in the two thousand years that separate them, Lasswell's model is more comprehensive than Aristotle's. For example, Lasswell was able to broaden the medium to include the mass media as well as face-to-face communication. Note that Aristotle's model does not include *effect*. For him, the only outcome of a persuasive message was that it would persuade the recipients to the communicator's point of view. By asking *with what effect?*, Lasswell suggests that there could be a variety of outcomes or effects of communication, some of which may be unintentional (refer to section 1.2.4).

1.4.4 Shannon and Weaver's view of communication

Shannon and Weaver worked for the Bell Telephone Laboratory in the United States. They were primarily

Figure 1.5: The Shannon and Weaver model (after Shannon & Weaver 1949)

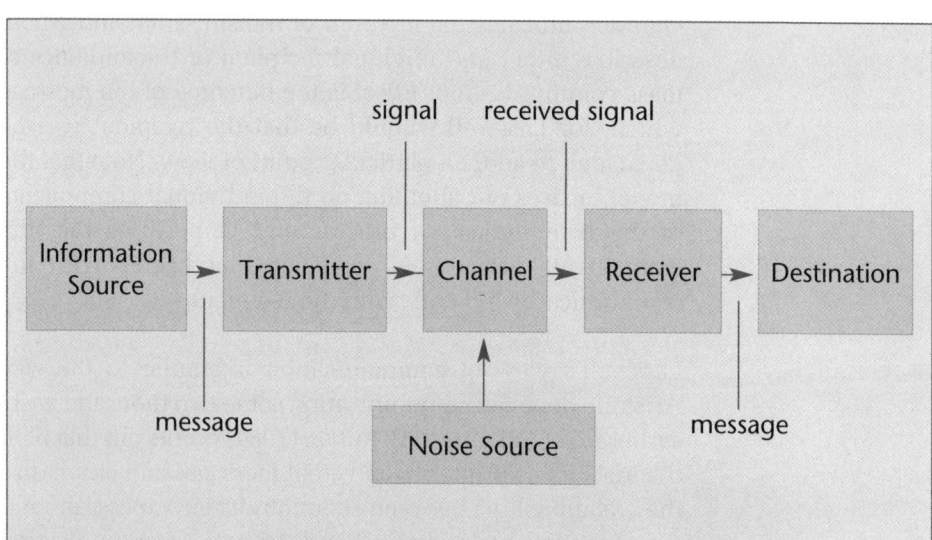

Shannon and Weaver's model

interested in finding engineering solutions to problems of signal transmission. They concentrated on how the channels of communication could be used most efficiently — how to send a maximum amount of information along a given channel. Think about the model in terms of how a telephone message is transmitted. An information source (communicator) encodes a message which is converted by the transmitter (telephone) into a signal which is sent through a channel (telephone line) to the receiver. The signal is received at the other end (telephone) and converted back into a message which is heard by the recipient (destination). Shannon and Weaver concentrated on which kind of communication channel carries the maximum amount of signals or sounds, how much of the signal is lost through noise (for example static on a telephone line) before it reaches its destination, and how to eliminate distortion caused by noise.

Bittner (1985) points out that the model describes mass communication as well. In radio broadcasting, for example, the announcer (information source) says words (the message) that are transmitted in the form of a radio wave (signal) to a radio receiver (receiver) which in turn would change the signal to an audible voice (the message) to be heard by the listener (destination) at home.

Like Lasswell's model, Shannon and Weaver's model depicts a sequential process in which each component of the communication process is clearly defined. Although not indicated by means of a label, Shannon and Weaver's model also draws our attention to the effects of the message — the effects of noise on the reception and understanding of the message by the recipient. This is because Shannon and Weaver's greatest concern was the efficient transmission of information from communicator to recipient and the clarity of the message that is transmitted. They did not consider the content of the message or the meaning that is conveyed and interpreted by the participants.

technical model

For this reason, Shannon and Weaver's model is often referred to as a transmission or ***technical model*** — it depicts the relationship between the communicator, message and recipient as a linear (one-way) process. Many subsequent theorists have maintained that the most important aspect of communication is the transmission process because, if the communicator's message does not reach the recipient without distortion, then little communication can take place between them (Ellis & McClintock 1994). Theorists who adopt a technical view of communication concentrate on improving the transmission process — the tools and techniques that help us to communicate more efficiently (refer to section 1.1).

Although it is technical, the model is considered important because it provided a basis for developing other models which deal more specifically with the process of **human** communication. When applied to human communication, Shannon and Weaver's model has several limitations or drawbacks. The first (and perhaps the greatest) limitation is that there is no channel for feedback (compare Lasswell's model). Secondly, it assumes that noise arises only in the channel; that is, it depicts only physical or external noise as a distortion in the communication process (refer to the discussion of noise in section 1.3.8). The third limitation follows from the second: the model is only concerned with the clarity of the message, and not with its meaning (McQuail & Windahl 1981). The scholar who first described communication as an interactive process was Wilbur Schramm.

1.4.5 Schramm's view of communication

Schramm's models

Schramm described three models, each showing a progression in his thoughts on communication. The first model is similar to Shannon and Weaver's. It is a technical model that follows the transmission of a message between communicator and recipient in a linear fashion without paying attention to the content of the message. However, Schramm's views are broader than those of Shannon and Weaver (and Lasswell), as the following quotation from his writings shows.

> A *source* may be an individual (speaking, writing, drawing, gesturing) or a communication organization (like a newspaper, publishing house, television station or motion picture studio). The *message* may be in the form

of ink on paper, sound waves in the air, impulses in electric current, a wave of the hand, a flag in the air, or any other signal capable of being interpreted meaningfully. The *destination* may be an *individual* listening, watching or reading; a member of a *group* such as a discussion group, a lecture audience, a football crowd, or a mob; or an individual member of a particular group we call the mass audience, such as the reader of a newspaper or a viewer of television. (Schramm 1954:3–4)

Figure 1.6: Schramm's first model

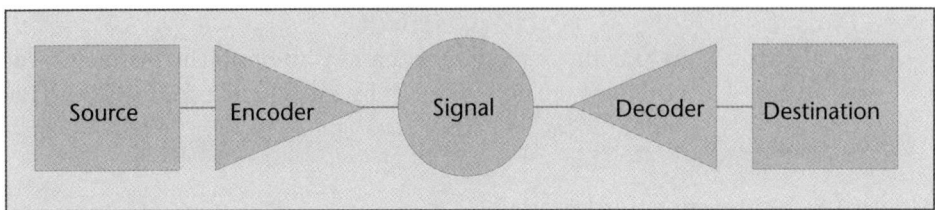

(Adapted from Schramm 1965)

Lasswell had already introduced the idea that the recipient of a message could be a single individual or a large audience. Schramm suggests that the *communicator* could also be either one person or an organisation such as a newspaper. In addition, Schramm broadens the medium to include any sign or signal that can carry a message, for instance a nonverbal sign.

Figure 1.7: Schramm's second model

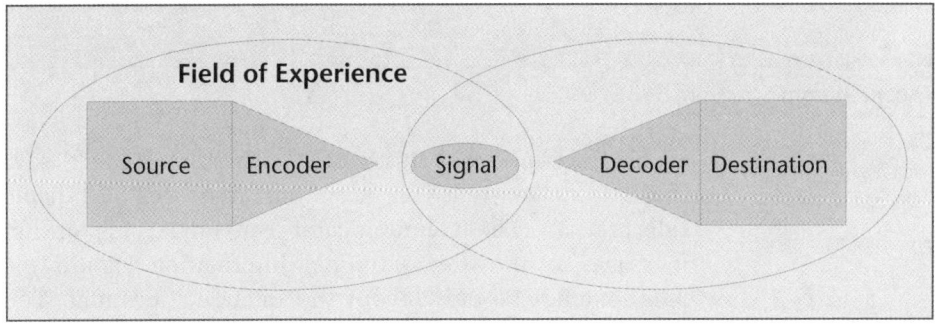

(Adapted from Schramm 1965)

fields of experience

In his description of the second model, Schramm introduces the term *fields of experience*. He was aware that, for a message to be understood by the recipient in the manner intended by the communicator, the participants must share a common language, common backgrounds and a common culture (Ruben 1984). (*Fields of experience* thus describes the conditions for interpretation we discuss in section 1.3.7.) Schramm is suggesting that, if people do not have some common background, noise (such as internal prejudices) may be introduced and cause misunderstanding or different interpretations of the message by the participants.

In the third model, Schramm attempts to overcome the problems created by noise by introducing feedback into the communication process.

Figure 1.8: Schramm's third model

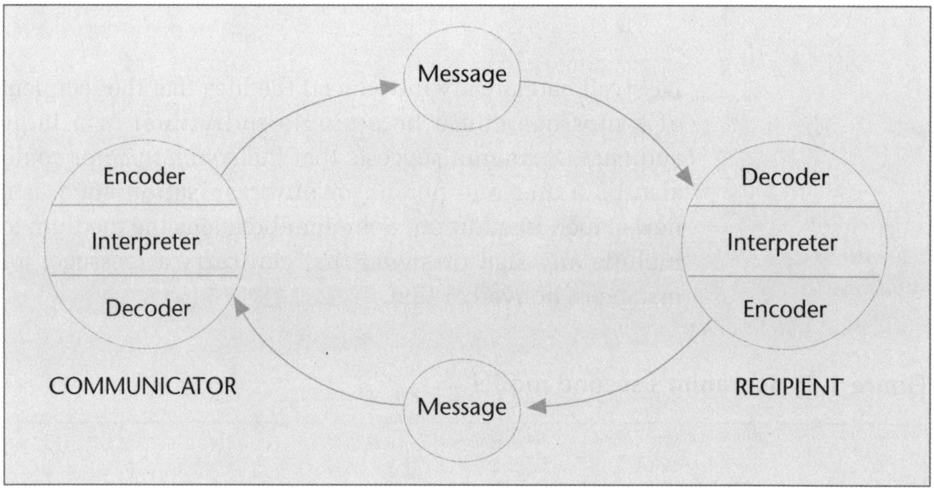

(Adapted from Schramm 1965)

In his description of this model, Schramm (1954:9) says that "feedback tells us how our messages are being interpreted". The communicator can adjust his or her message, or provide additional information should the recipient not be clear about the intended meaning. You may already have realised that the progression in thought revealed in Schramm's models moves away from the technical view of communication to the issue of the content of messages and the meaning that is exchanged between the participants. Schramm and other theorists who follow this approach to the study of communication regard *meaning*, not transmission, as the most important aspect of the communication process. They maintain that, even if a message is transmitted and received clearly and accurately, its meaning may not be understood in the same way by the participants because they may not share similar circumstances (or fields of experience) (Ellis & McClintock 1994). Unlike Shannon and Weaver, they do not believe that there is only one correct meaning for a message. The meaning is determined by the person who is interpreting it (refer to the discussion of interpretation in section 1.3.7).

Schramm's view of communication is more complex than previous views and adds substantially to our understanding of the communication process. Schramm's model describes communication as a dynamic interaction in which meaningful messages are exchanged by two active participants. Communicator and recipient both encode, transmit, receive, decode and interpret messages — that is, both play the roles of communicator and recipient. By highlighting the importance of feedback, the process becomes two-way instead of linear. The model thus moves away from emphasising the channel through which messages are transmitted to the **interpretation of meaning** by the people in the process.

1.4.6   A transactional model

By identifying the components and relationships basic to the communication process, the early models we have discussed laid a foundation on which future scholars could build. The model below (figure 1.9) uses all the elements in the previous models and builds on them to show that communication does not only involve the transmission of messages from one person to another, nor is it simply an interaction between two people. The communication process becomes a *transaction* during which the meaning of a message is negotiated (refer to the definitions in section 1.1). At the same time, the transactional model overcomes the major limitation in Schramm's model — that is, the suggestion that communicator and recipient take turns to express and interpret messages.

Figure 1.9: A transactional model of communication

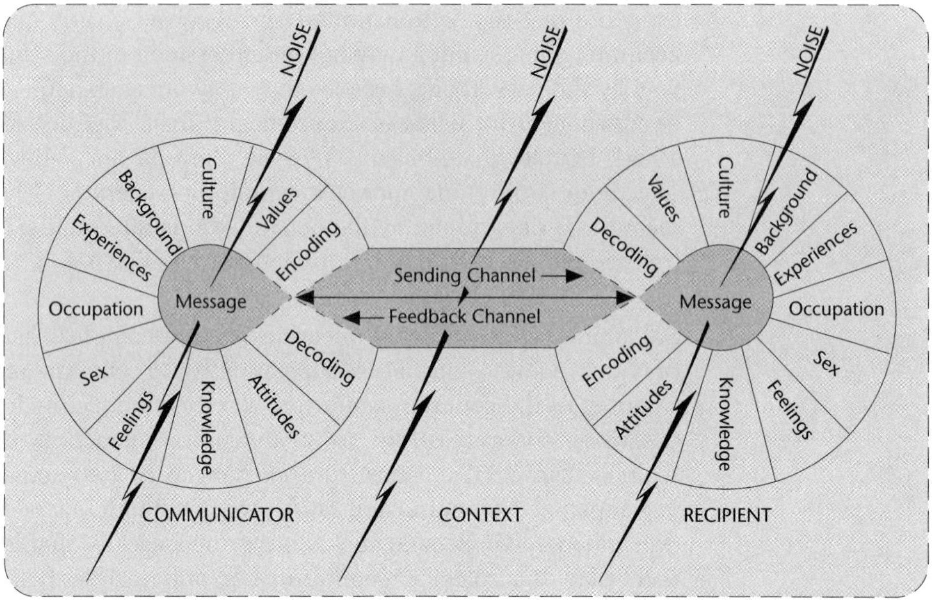

(Adapted from Verderber 1990)

transactional model

The model is not substantially different from the circular model — it also depicts communication as a dynamic process in which both participants are actively engaged in encoding, transmitting, receiving and decoding messages. The main difference is that communication is seen within the context of a relationship between two participants who are **simultaneously** involved in the **negotiation** of meaning. Simultaneous implies that, instead of a two-way flow, both people are constantly encoding and decoding messages. For example, even as I talk to you, I am watching your nonverbal reactions and interpreting them so that there is, in fact, no longer a separation between the two communicators (Tubbs & Moss 1991).

The transactional model also highlights that the creation of meaning is **negotiated** between the participants. The two circles represent the communicator and the recipient. In the centre of each circle is the message: the thought, idea or feeling that is communicated using verbal and nonverbal signs. Surrounding the messages are the participants' values, culture, background, occupation, sex, values, interests, knowledge and attitudes. These factors influence the meaning that is expressed and the meaning that is interpreted. The outcome of the encounter is determined by the mutual involvement of the participants in negotiating the meaning of the messages.

The bar between the circles represents the medium of communication. Rather than depicting transmission and feedback as two separate processes (compare Schramm's model), the transactional model indicates that messages are continually passing between the participants. The area around the communicator and the recipient represents the context or circumstances in which the process takes place. While it is taking place, external, internal and semantic noise may be occurring at various places in the model. These noises may affect the ability of communicator and recipient to share meanings.

We would not like to leave you with the impression that the models we have selected are the only models in the literature on communication. As we explained earlier, our purpose has been to illustrate different ways of conceptualising the communication process. The development of communication models has continued until the present time and reflects the increasingly broad range of topics covered in communication studies. We would like to encourage you to study other communication models yourself by referring to the suggested reading list at the end of this unit.

As the focus of communication studies broadened, the way in which communication was studied also began to change. One of the important developments has been a move away from general models and theories which try to explain a wide range of communication situations to an approach that deals with specific contexts of communication. In the next section, we introduce some of the contexts which are receiving attention from communication scholars today. Later on in this module we deal with these contexts in greater detail.

1.5 Contextual approaches to communication

Think for a moment about your own experience of communication. For example, in a single day you may have a conversation with a friend, engage in deep thoughts, listen to the radio, read the newspaper, look at an illustrated pamphlet, participate in a seminar, make a speech to a business or social group, watch television, or go to the cinema. Each of these experiences occurs in different situations, involves different numbers of people, uses different means of communication, and creates different relationships.

contexts

Contexts are different types of communication situation or setting classified according to the number of people involved in them and the degree to which they are able to interact. The settings are: intrapersonal communication, interpersonal communication, small-group communi-cation, organisational communication, public speaking and mass communication. The contexts are not mutually exclusive and the distinctions among them are not clear-cut. Note that the degree to which people are able to interact refers to the immediacy of feedback they are able to provide. In other words, is feedback possible and, if so, is it immediately available or delayed?

1.5.1 The intrapersonal communication context

intrapersonal communication

The term *intra* means 'within' or 'inside'. **Intrapersonal communication** occurs when an individual sends and receives messages internally: in other words, you communicate with yourself. The distinguishing charac-teristic of intrapersonal communication is that you are the only participant — you are the communicator-recipient. The message is made up of your thoughts and feelings which your brain processes and interprets. Feedback occurs in the sense that, as you 'talk' to yourself, you make decisions, or discard some ideas and replace them with others (Hybels & Weaver 1995). Intrapersonal communication is an ongoing process that is taking place even while you are communicating in all the other settings. For instance, you are probably doing it right now, since thinking about what you are reading is a form of intrapersonal communication. Intrapersonal communication is the foundation on which interpersonal communication is based. To communicate effectively with others, you first have to be able to communicate with yourself. Communication theorists have investigated the way people make sense of the world through their intrapersonal communication. We discuss intrapersonal communication in more detail in unit 3.

1.5.2 The interpersonal communication context

interpersonal communication

The term *inter* means 'between'. **Interpersonal communication** occurs between people in a face-to-face situation. They are able to see each other and observe facial expressions and other nonverbal behaviour while they are exchanging verbal messages. A characteristic of interpersonal communication is that the participants continually provide feedback or respond to each other's messages. Conversing with your sister, discussing a movie with your friends, or talking to your boss or your teacher are examples of interpersonal communication. As you can see from these examples, this kind of communication is usually between two people, though it may include more than two. It is in the interpersonal context that meaningful relationships are formed and maintained in our daily interactions with others. Relationships are the focus of study in the interpersonal context. We discuss interpersonal communication in more detail in unit 4.

1.5.3 The small-group communication context

small-group communication

Small-group communication refers to communication within a group of between three and twelve people. The group must be small enough so that each member is able to interact with all the other members. We all belong to a number of groups: the family, work groups, social clubs, church groups, study groups, and so forth. People in groups usually share a common purpose or goal which brings them together, such as the need to solve a problem. Small-group communication is also interpersonal because the members of the group are able to interact with each other by providing feedback, but it is more complex than communication between two people because groups have unique dynamics that affect the way people interact. Small-group communication is the topic of unit 5.

1.5.4 The organisational communication context

organisational communication

Organisational communication developed as a specialisation area in the field of communication studies in the late 1940s and early 1950s as a response to the need for organisations to become more efficient and productive in order to serve the needs of society. Organisational communication is important in businesses and industrial organisations as well as in churches, hospitals, government agencies, military organisations and academic institutions. Members of an organisation communicate as individuals and in groups, and can be called upon to deliver oral presentations. The interests of organisational communication include the flow of information within the organisation and between the organisation and society; how communication skills can be used to help people succeed in the organisation; leadership ability and management styles; and the quality of interpersonal relationships within the organisation. Organisational communication is discussed in unit 6.

1.5.5 The public speaking context

public speaking

When the group becomes too large for direct interaction between the members, we talk about the ***public speaking*** context or an oral presentation. In public speaking one person addresses an audience in a public setting such as a lecture hall or auditorium. Public speaking is more formal than interpersonal or small-group communication. Usually the event is planned in advance, the speaker is introduced, and delivers a speech that has been prepared to meet the goals of the particular situation. It could be a persuasive political speech, a presentation by a salesperson to promote the company's products, a lecture to students, or a speech at a wedding. Participants are still face to face but the audience does not usually participate directly until the end of the speech when questions are invited. However, they can send nonverbal messages or feedback. An audience that is not enjoying a speech, for instance, often becomes restless and stops paying attention. They can also provide positive feedback in the form of laughter or applause. We do not deal any further with public speaking in this introductory text because it is the topic of a separate book in this series, *Persuasive communication skills: public speaking* (Steinberg 1999).

1.5.6   The mass communication context

mass communication

Mass communication is communication to large masses of people who do not know each other and who are usually not in the same place. A distinguishing characteristic of mass communication is that it is mediated — that is, the message reaches you through a mechanical or electronic medium such as print or television. When you read a book, watch a movie, or listen to the news on the radio, for instance, you are part of a mass communication audience. Mass communication differs from interpersonal and group communication in many ways. An important difference is that it provides little or no opportunity for you to interact directly with the person or people conveying the message due to the difficulty of providing feedback. Areas of study include the influence of mass communication on people's behaviour, and the way exposure to the mass media shapes our perceptions of the world. You will learn more about mass communication in unit 7.

FOUNDATIONS OF COMMUNICATION STUDY **39**

Case 1.1

This case is adapted from Verderber (1990).

The chairperson at a business meeting looks at her watch and sees that there are only five minutes left before she has to leave for a lunch-time appointment with the bank manager. She frowns because there are still two items on the agenda that have not been dealt with. Aware that it is too late to begin a discussion, she says, "Let's call it a day," in a frustrated tone of voice. Some members of the group look surprised because meetings in that organisation usually carry on until all business has been completed, regardless of the time. Others smile because, for a change, the meeting is not going to run into the lunch hour. Most people gather their notebooks and pens and begin leaving. John, however, looks confused — he has been thinking about the argument he had with his girlfriend the previous evening.

After you have studied this case, answer the following questions.

1. Identify the context in which the communication takes place.

2. Is the context formal or informal?

3. How many communication codes are used? Substantiate your answer by means of examples.

4. Identify the channel(s) of communication.

5. What message is the chairperson communicating?

6. Do you think there is an example of unintentional communication? Explain your answer.

7. Give three examples of feedback by the recipients.

8. Has noise interfered in the communication process? Explain.

9. Does the case describe a technical or meaning-centred view of communication?

Summary

We started this unit by describing communication as a complex phenomenon. We first considered three definitions of communication: a technical definition, an interactive

---

definition and a transactional definition. We then extended our understanding of the complex nature of communication by examining the following dimensions of communication: verbal and nonverbal communication, oral and written communication, formal and informal communication, and intentional and unintentional communication. In the next part of the unit we described, with the aid of examples, the components or elements that comprise the process of communication. This was followed by a discussion of communication models to illustrate three different ways of conceptualising the communication process: linear, interactional (process) and transactional models. We continued with a brief description of the different contexts in which communication is studied today: intrapersonal communication, interpersonal communication, small-group communication, organisational communication, public speaking and mass communication. We ended the unit with a case study which describes the communication process among the members of an organisation.

Test-yourself

1   Think about a serious conversation or an argument you have had recently with a friend or family member. Write down your experience using all the components discussed in section 1.3 in this book to describe the interaction. Then answer the following questions.

   (a)   Did you both participate actively in the encounter?

   (b)   Did you both make yourselves understood?

   (c)   Did your partner's nonverbal communication help you to understand him/her more easily?

   (d)   Did your encounter have a satisfactory outcome? (Why or why not?)

   (e)   Was it disturbed by any kind of noise? (What kind of noise and what effect did it have?)

2   Working either on your own, or with a fellow student, develop an original model of the one-to-one communication process. Try to include all the components that comprise and influence the process, and label each part.

3   Think about the different views of communication we have described and how each changes the way in which the concept of communication is understood. Then formulate your own definition, emphasising the aspects of communication you consider to be important. Would you say that your definition offers a technical or a meaning-centred view of communication?

4   Define six settings in which communication takes place. Explain the basis on which we differentiate between the settings, illustrating your answers with examples from your own experience of communication.

Suggested reading

Barker, LL & Gaut, DA. 1996. *Communication.* 7th edition. Boston: Allyn & Bacon.

Dimbleby, R & Burton, G. 1992. *More than words: an introduction to communication.* 2nd edition. London: Routledge.

Du Plooy, GM. 1991. *500 communication concepts.* Cape Town: Juta.

Ellis, R & McClintock, A. 1994. *If you take my meaning: theory and practice in human communication.* 2nd edition. London: Edward Arnold.

Hybels, S & Weaver, RL. 1995. *Communicating effectively.* 4th edition. New York: Random House.

McQuail, D & Windahl, S. 1981. *Communication models for the study of mass communications.* New York: Longman.

Verderber, RF & Verderber, KS. 1992. *Interact: using interpersonal communication skills.* 6th edition. Belmont: Wadsworth.

Nonverbal communication

Overview

It's the first day of a new job and you want to make a good impression. You have set the alarm clock for earlier than usual so that you will have plenty of time to prepare for the day. After a shower, you take particular care about the clothes you choose — not too casual, but not too smart either — you don't want your new colleagues to think that your appearance is more suitable for a cocktail party than for a day at the office. As you leave, you check your hair in the mirror and collect the articles you have selected to put in your office — a photograph taken at your graduation ceremony, a dictionary, a pencil box and a pot plant.

The description we have outlined may seem pretty routine, but as Staley and Staley (1992) point out, your actions reveal a great deal about yourself without a single word being uttered. Your concern about being punctual, the care that you have taken to make a good first impression, and even the items you place in your office, all communicate nonverbal messages that speak as loudly as words. To arrive at a better understanding of communication and to develop skills that allow more effective participation in the communication process, you need to be aware of the range of nonverbal signs you are conveying and receiving at a particular time. The ability to analyse nonverbal messages enhances your understanding of other people's meaning and helps to eliminate communication problems. In addition, how people are perceived as communicators is based partly on their use of nonverbal skills.

In this unit, we provide a framework for understanding the role and impact of your own and other people's nonverbal communication. After defining the term *nonverbal communication*, we explain the functions of nonverbal communication and then go on to discuss some of the factors that influence our understanding of our own and other people's nonverbal behaviour, such as the context of the communication encounter and the culture of the participants. We continue with a discussion of six categories of nonverbal behaviour and then suggest how you can apply what you have learned to your own communication. We end the unit with a case study which is based on examples of nonverbal communication in a printed publication.

Learning outcomes

At the end of this unit you should be able to do the following.

1 Define *nonverbal communication* and identify the reasons for studying it.

2 Describe five functions of nonverbal communication using examples from your everyday experience of communication.

3 Explain three factors that influence our understanding of nonverbal communication.

4 Describe the relationship between verbal and nonverbal communication.

5 Explain the meaning of the following categories of nonverbal communication and illustrate each with an example from your own experience: *kinesics, proxemics, haptics, chronemics, personal appearance* and *paralanguage.*

6 Apply what you have learned about nonverbal communication in everyday experiences of communication.

7 Be more sensitive to your own use of nonverbal messages.

8 Answer the questions based on the case at the end of this unit.

Introduction

As we explained in unit 1, the term *nonverbal* is commonly used to describe all intentional and unintentional messages that are not written or spoken. But nonverbal communication is not only concerned with the image that people present through personal appearance or interior design as in the scenario described in the Overview. It is also concerned with messages we send through our body movements, gestures, facial expressions, tone of voice, and eye behaviour, as well as our use of space, time and touch. In fact, researchers report that, in face-to-face communication, more than 65 per cent of the meaning in a message is conveyed by nonverbal behaviour (Mehrabian 1981; Stewart 1990). Your own experience tells you that, at times, you are at a loss when you need words to express feelings and emotions. When a person needs comforting, for example, a touch or a smile is often more effective than words. Nonverbal communication also has an effect even when the participants are not in each other's presence. In a telephone conversation, for example, some of the meaning of a message is carried by the speaker's tone of voice. Very often, the success of your communication and relationships depends on how well you 'read' these silent messages from others. To gain greater insight into the complexities of nonverbal behaviour, we begin by discussing the functions that nonverbal communication serves.

2.1 Functions of nonverbal communication

We learn about the functions of nonverbal messages by studying them in relationship to verbal messages: how do they affect verbal messages? Essentially, a nonverbal message functions in one of five ways: it reinforces, complements, contradicts, replaces or regulates a verbal message (Knapp 1990; Verderber 1990).

reinforce/accent

A nonverbal message **reinforces** or **accents** the verbal message when it adds to its meaning. In the same way that underlining or *italicising* written words emphasises them, saying "Come here **now**" conveys a more urgent message than "Come here now". Pounding your hand on the table when saying, "Listen to me!", conveys a more effective message than the words alone. While your gesture may be redundant, it adds emphasis to your statement and captures the listener's attention. Very often, reinforcing the message is not deliberate; it is done without conscious thought or intent on our part (Verderber 1990).

complement

A nonverbal message **complements** the verbal message when it conveys the same meaning. If you tell someone, "I'm pleased to meet you", and accompany it with a warm smile, your tone of voice and facial expression are complementing the verbal message.

contradict

A nonverbal message may **contradict** the verbal message. People often say one thing, but do another — for example, the student about to make an oral presentation to the class who says, "I'm not nervous", despite his trembling hands and perspiring forehead. Research has shown that, in most cases, people tend to believe the nonverbal cues rather than the words that are spoken. Nonverbal messages are highly credible, perhaps because they often convey feelings and emotions. The voice may also contradict the verbal message. A change in pitch, for example, can tell us that someone is perhaps telling a lie or being sarcastic or merely teasing. Research has shown that when we are attempting to conceal the truth, our pitch tends to change in an upward direction and lets others know that we are contradicting the verbal message (Barker & Gaut 1996).

replace

A nonverbal message may **replace** the verbal message. Gestures, facial expressions and other nonverbal cues generate meaning without the use of words. You wave your hand to someone instead of saying hello, or give someone a hug instead of saying "thanks for helping me" — your message is clear. Similarly, the expression on the face of a dejected person who comes home after a hard day at work substitutes for the statement "I've had a rotten day".

regulate

Nonverbal behaviour functions to **regulate** the flow of verbal interaction. Your eye contact, tone of voice, nodding of the head, slight hand movements, and other nonverbal behaviour tell your partner when to talk, to repeat a statement, to hurry up, or to finish the conversation. Good public speakers learn to adjust what they are saying and how they are saying it on the basis of such cues from the audience. The same applies to group communication. The chairperson at a meeting, for example, uses eye contact or hand gestures instead of words to indicate whose turn it is to speak.

2.2 Aspects of nonverbal communication

Before we discuss nonverbal communication in more detail, we need to be aware that the potential for misunderstanding a nonverbal message is greater than for misunderstanding a verbal message. To begin with, nonverbal communication is often beyond our control. Whereas we can plan what we say very carefully and stop talking at will, we cannot simply 'switch off' nonverbal behaviour. Even if we consciously control our facial expression and hand movements to hide the fact that we are nervous, for example, our strained voice or shaking knees may give us away. We call such nonverbal cues **leakage** because we are in fact leaking information about ourselves that we cannot hide (Burton & Dimbleby 1995). Nonverbal behaviour confirms the **axiom** that "One cannot *not* communicate" (Watzlawick, Beavin & Jackson 1968:51). Even your silence communicates a message, and you cannot tell your body not to leak information by way of your posture, for example, or the clothes you are wearing.

leakage

axiom
a generally
accepted
statement

context

Another factor that has to be taken into account is that nonverbal behaviour is **contextual**. We said earlier that verbal and nonverbal signs work together to convey the total meaning of a message. Whereas verbal communication primarily conveys content information, nonverbal communication primarily conveys relational information (emotions and feelings), depending on the circumstances or context in which it occurs (refer back to unit 1). The tone of voice of the communicator, for example, can convey sincerity or sarcasm, depending on how the message is related to the circumstances. "Nice work" is a compliment when you have completed a difficult project, but a reprimand when you submit a careless piece of work. Similarly, you know from your own experience that smiles, nods and winks can convey different meanings, depending on the context in which we find ourselves.

Whether the context is formal or informal also plays a role in determining nonverbal behaviour. While you might watch television at home with your feet up on a table, you are unlikely to do so at someone else's home unless invited to 'make yourself comfortable'. Similarly, you might pick up some food from your plate with your fingers at home, but are less likely to do so at a dinner party. We hope that some of you reacted spontaneously to the latter example by saying, "That's not a valid statement. In my culture, it's perfectly acceptable to eat with one's fingers at a dinner party." This example shows that one of the major causes of misunderstanding between people of different cultures is the assumption that nonverbal cues have the same meaning for all parties.

culture

We are often unaware of the pervasive influence that *culture* has on the meaning we attach to nonverbal communication. Each culture provides its members with a code of behaviour that is acceptable in different situations. Most of our nonverbal communication is learned in the same way. Research results suggest that some aspects of nonverbal communication seem to be fairly consistent, regardless of race or culture. For example, studies have shown that facial expressions to convey emotions such as fear, surprise, happiness or anger are relatively constant across cultures and are thus fairly easy to recognise and interpret. But more subtle facial expressions like disgust, surprise or embarrassment may vary across cultures (Ellis & McClintock 1994). In North America, embarrassment, for instance, is normally shown by blushing; in Japan, embarrassment is shown by laughter and giggling; Arabs show embarrassment by sticking out their tongues slightly (Hamilton & Parker 1990). Similarly, the signs given by clothing may be personal or influenced by the culture of the individual. As a result there may be more variation in the way such signs are interpreted. In South Africa, a woman dressed entirely in black is signifying that she is a widow, whereas a woman wearing a black pinafore is communicating the loss of a child. Attaching fixed meanings to nonverbal signs without taking the cultural context into account often results in misunderstanding and the creation of **stereotypes**. (We discuss stereotypes in more detail in section 3.4.1.) In a multicultural country such as South Africa, it becomes even more important to be aware that all nonverbal communication conveys information that must be evaluated or interpreted within the context in which it occurs.

> **stereotype**
> a standardised image of a type of person

2.3 Categories of nonverbal communication

Before you begin your study of the categories of nonverbal behaviour, we would like you to be aware that it could be extremely misleading to try to make a list of nonverbal signs and attach a single meaning to each, as many popular books on 'body language' tend to do. There is no dictionary for understanding nonverbal behaviour. Because nonverbal messages are more ambiguous than verbal messages, they do not always mean what people think they do. The real reason that someone constantly glances at the clock during a meeting, for example, may not be that he is bored, but because he is expecting an important phone call.

We discuss the following categories of nonverbal communication: kinesics, proxemics, haptics, chronemics, personal appearance and paralanguage. The discussion is based largely on research about nonverbal communication that has been published in North America and Britain. Therefore, many of the assumptions and examples of nonverbal communication pertain to Western cultures. As you read the discussion, please feel free to disagree with any assertions we make if they do not coincide with the meanings of a particular nonverbal sign in your culture.

2.3.1 Kinesics

> **kinesics**

Body movement, gestures, posture, facial expressions and eye contact fall within the broad field of nonverbal study called **kinesics**. The term was coined by Ray Birdwhistell

(1952, 1970), a pioneer in this field of study. He was among the first theorists to suggest that communication is not restricted to verbal language, and that there is a significant connection between physical behaviour and spoken language. Birdwhistell concluded that body movements could be studied and understood like a language such as English or Tswana, and he made an intensive study of how people infer or attribute meaning to physical signs in their communication encounters.

body movements

Body movements are strong indicators of how you feel. Have you ever considered how much you communicate about yourself simply by the way you walk? Watch the people walking down a busy street. Some, for example, walk as though they are in a daze and seem oblivious to what is going on around them, whereas others stride along as if they are determined and confident about where they are going. An interesting study conducted in the United States shows that people in the first category are more likely to be mugged than those in the second! Their body movements seem to communicate to potential muggers that they could be easy prey (Wilson, Hantz & Hanna 1989).

On a more scientific basis, researchers Ekman and Friesen (1969) have classified body movements into five classes: emblems, illustrators, regulators, affect displays, and body manipulators. Let's look at examples of each.

Figure 2.1: Can you understand these emblems?

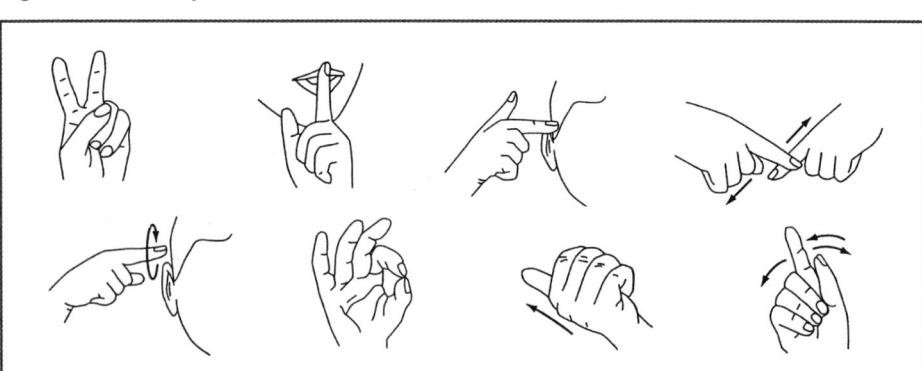

(Adapted from Barker & Gaut 1996:81)

emblems

Emblems are nonverbal signs that have a direct translation into words, for instance the sign language of the deaf, the extended thumb of the hitchhiker, and the two-fingered peace symbol. Unlike much of our nonverbal behaviour, emblems are intentional and are most often used when verbal channels are blocked or impractical — for example, when people are too far apart to make themselves heard. In other words, they substitute for or replace the verbal message. For example, you knock on your neighbour's door, and, because she is on the telephone, she waves a greeting to you and then gestures for you to come in and sit down. However, some emblems are not universal and their meanings have to be learned within each culture. For example, an investigation which tested twenty emblems revealed that a gesture that was intended to signify good luck/be well (*sterkte/voorspoed*) was interpreted **differently** by Afrikaans-, Tswana- and Southern Sotho-speaking respondents (Terblanche 1994).

illustrators

Illustrators are the aptly named nonverbal sketches or pictures that accent, emphasise or reinforce words. Examples are gestures that illustrate the shape or size of an object, such as the large fish that you caught, as well as the hand movements that illustrate the directions you might give someone about how to reach a particular destination. They are usually intentional and are often used in situations where the verbal code alone is unable to convey meaning accurately — they help to make communication more exact. Because illustrators are more universal than emblems, they are less likely to cause misunderstanding.

affect displays

Affect displays are facial expressions of emotion. The face is a constant source of information to those around us. Facial expressions communicate emotional states or reactions to a message and generally mirror the intensity of people's thoughts and feelings. Examples include smiling, frowning, lifting the eyebrows, and pursing the lips. Although it is not always possible to interpret all facial expressions correctly, they can be a more accurate cue to interpreting people's emotions than the words they use. Apart from the universal facial expressions of anger, fear and happiness discussed above, it has been estimated that the face is capable of producing more than 20 000 expressions (Staley & Staley 1992). Combinations of emotions — anger plus fear, for example — make matters even more complicated. Unlike emblems and illustrators, affect displays are almost impossible to control, making your face the primary means for communicating emotions.

regulators

Regulators are the subtle signs we use to control the give-and-take of conversation (refer to section 2.1). All of these signals are sent quickly and almost unconsciously, and are an effective means of assisting the exchange of listening and speaking roles in a communication encounter. Regulators include head nods, puzzled looks, and changes in posture. The teacher who points to the child she wants to answer the question is using a regulator.

adaptors

Adaptors are nonverbal ways of adjusting to a communication situation. They can also be described as movements designed to meet physical or emotional needs. Have you noticed that when people feel self-conscious, they tend to straighten their clothes and pat their hair? It seems to help relieve tension, or reduce the stress experienced by, for example, a public speaker. Rubbing your eyes, jingling the change in your pocket, fiddling with your jewellery, or biting your fingernails are also examples of adaptors.

posture

Posture also communicates a great deal of information about yourself. The way you sit, stand, slump or slouch provides information about your gender, status, self-image, attitudes and emotional state. Slouching or sitting with your hands on your head often indicates that you are feeling low, whereas sitting with your feet on the desk may be interpreted by others as a sign of your feeling of superiority.

gestures

Gestures are movements of hands, legs, arms and feet. People vary in the amount of gesturing they use. Hand gestures are commonly used to describe or emphasise a verbal description or to communicate attitudes. For example, in a conversation, crossing your arms generally conveys a less aggressive attitude than putting your hands on your hips. Similarly, leaning forward usually conveys a positive attitude towards the other person, while leaning backwards could be interpreted negatively.

eye contact

Eye contact is another aspect of nonverbal communication which helps us to interpret meaning. Eye contact refers to the way we use our eyes to regulate and monitor the effects of communication. For example, public speakers who never look up convey the impression that they are nervous. Speakers who do look at their audience during a speech come across as confident and in control. However, unlike some facial expressions, the use of eye contact is a less universal convention. In some traditional African cultures, for example, dropping your eyes in conversation with a superior is regarded as a sign of respect, whereas in Western cultures little or no eye contact is often interpreted as an indication of boredom, a lack of concentration, or a feeling of inferiority. Even though conventions in eye contact may differ, it plays an important part in nonverbal behaviour and is something we learn in childhood as part of our cultural experience (Ellis & McClintock 1994).

2.3.2 Proxemics

proxemics

The study of how people's perception of space communicates information is known as ***proxemics***. The term was invented by Edward Hall (1969), who conducted cross-cultural studies on the use of space in personal and social situations. Proxemics includes the messages people convey when, for instance, they choose to sit at the front or back of a classroom, or whether they sit near to or far from the head of the table at a meeting. Most teachers will tell you that the mischief-makers dash to the back of the classroom and that the more serious students choose a front seat. Similarly, the general interpretation of people who sit far from the head of a table at a meeting is that they are reluctant to participate in the proceedings by voicing opinions. The danger of such fixed interpretations is that we often attribute the same generalisation to the person who may simply be late and occupies the only remaining empty seat.

Degrees of status are also communicated through the use of space. Heads of companies, university principals and high government officials usually have large, well-furnished offices, whereas their employees occupy smaller, more sparsely furnished spaces. In a household, children have smaller bedrooms than their parents, and often have to share that space with other family members.

The distance between people in communication conveys information about their relationship. Hall (1969) identified four spatial zones of interpersonal communication: intimate distance, personal distance, social distance and public distance. The basic premise of his theory is that when we observe the distance that people maintain between themselves and others in interpersonal communication, we can tell which people have close relationships and which have formal relationships. Hall found that the use of space depends on your nationality and culture. The findings below apply to the meanings that most Western cultures ascribe to space.

Figure 2.2: The four distance zones

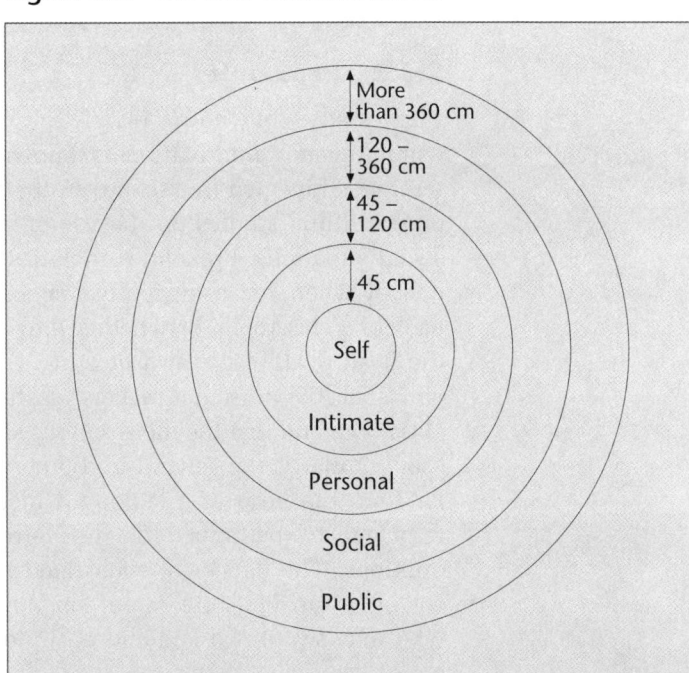

intimate distance

In *intimate distance*, people are in direct contact with each other or are no more than 45 centimetres apart. It is the zone reserved for lovemaking and only those who are very close to you are allowed into it. Most people feel apprehensive when those who have no right to be there

personal distance

intrude into it. In *personal distance* people are between 45–120 centimetres from each other. This is the distance most often reserved for interactions with friends or family members. It is close enough to see each others' reactions, but far enough away not to encroach on their intimate zone.

When people do not know each other very well, they tend

social distance

to maintain a *social distance* of 120–360 centimetres. This is the distance most often used at social gatherings, business meetings or interviews. A distance of more than

public distance

360 centimetres or *public distance* is typically used in public speaking situations. It indicates a formal occasion such as a politician addressing a gathering. At this distance, there is little opportunity for mutual involvement in the communication encounter.

Look at the photograph reproduced in figure 2.6. What does it tell you about the distances people maintain in personal and social situations?

Space influences what we talk about with others. You would be considered rather odd and certainly very rude if you entered someone's intimate zone to ask the time. Likewise, it would be difficult to have a conversation of a personal nature with someone at a social distance — apart from the fact that everyone else in the vicinity would be able to overhear your conversation, the distance is too great to provide a setting which is conducive to exchanging confidences (Hybels & Weaver 1989).

While all individuals have spatial zones, Hall established that the distance of the zones varies across cultures. People of different cultures have different notions about, for example, what is considered an appropriate distance between strangers. Generally, Latin Americans, Arabs, Turks and Italians converse at a closer distance than British

Figure 2.3: Personal and social distance zones

(Reproduced with the kind permission of Philip Schedler.)

people or North Americans (Shuter 1984). The way that different cultures use space could create problems if, for instance, you feel crowded by someone of another culture whom you feel is too close for comfort, whereas he or she might interpret your use of space as an indication that you are cold and distant.

2.3.3 Haptics

haptics

The field of study that examines messages that are conveyed by our use of touch is called **haptics**. Physical contact with others is the most basic form of communication and a lack of touch in certain situations often communicates that there is a problem. Social workers, for instance, know that something is wrong in a relationship when a parent avoids touching and hugging his or her child. Lack of contact in childhood often may also contribute to physical and psychological problems in adulthood. As with distance, touch communicates information about the nature of the relationship between people. Lovers usually touch each other more frequently in conversation than do friends. People who have just been introduced shake hands more formally than relatives. We often pat someone on the back to calm him or her down if he or she is angry. We may grab someone's elbow to attract his or her attention. Most of us also get pleasure from touching material objects — stroking the smooth leather of a pair of gloves or the silky feel of a dress or shirt.

Whether or not you often reach out to touch other people is often determined by cultural influences. Before making inferences about other people's use of touch, you should bear in mind that the kind of touching behaviour that is permissible in interpersonal communication depends largely on the individual's culture. Staley and Staley (1992) point out that we need to be especially careful about how we use haptics in an organisational environment. Aside from handshakes or the occasional pat on the back, touching your colleagues — no matter how innocently — may be misinterpreted as a sign of romantic attraction, and could result in a charge of sexual harassment.

2.3.4 Chronemics

chronemics

Chronemics is the field of study that is concerned with the use of time. Should your doorbell ring at three o'clock in the morning, for instance, your first thought is probably that something must be wrong. You have interpreted the meaning of the ringing doorbell in terms of time. If you leave a message for a friend to return a telephone call and he or she does not respond for three days, how do you interpret his or her action? Perhaps you will feel that your friendship is not as valuable to him or her as you thought. Again, time affected your interpretation of a message. Time influences the way we interpret many messages and forms of behaviour. Time is often a reflection of status: the higher our status, the more control we have over time. Parents control when their children will eat, bath and go to bed. Professionals in our society often control how long we wait for an appointment. As a student, you have little control of the date of an examination or the time of a particular class.

In most industrial societies (such as North America, Japan, Germany, South Africa) time is money and high productivity features prominently in the way of life of the society. People are intolerant of others who are consistently late for work or for appointments, and consider them to be both rude and irresponsible. But this inflexible conception of time does not apply to every society.

Some cultures have a more flexible attitude to time and misunderstandings can arise when people of different cultures conduct business and do not understand one another's assumptions about appropriate timing. In the same way, employers and employees of different cultures are often confused by the other's conception of punctuality.

2.3.5 Personal appearance

appearance

Why do people spend large sums of money each year on beauty products, weight control pills, make-up, new hair-styles and clothes? Some even resort to plastic surgery to increase their physical attractiveness. Why do most (Western) advertisements portray young, thin, attractive women and well-built, handsome men? Simply because we are judged by the way society has determined we should look. Physical appearance influences first impressions, job interviews, consumer buying behaviour, and even courtroom decisions.

While we may have no control over elements such as height or premature balding or the shape of our nose, elements over which we do have some control include clothing, hairstyle, jewellery, and so forth. Your appearance provides visual clues to your age, gender, status, personality and attitudes. For example, if you are inappropriately dressed at a job interview in a formal company, the interviewer may pay little attention to your qualifications because your appearance conveys the wrong message: jeans and a T-shirt indicate that your attitude is not right for the job! The interviewer, of course, is guilty of stereotyping and may be entirely wrong, but the damage has been done.

Appearance is considered so important in the business world that many large organisations have a strict dress code which lays down rules for the style and colour of clothing that may be worn, as well as the personal grooming of their employees. Others require their employees to wear uniforms that communicate to the public the image the organisation would like to portray.

Since your appearance conveys messages, you need to be aware of what is considered appropriate and what will be of most benefit to your image in both work and social situations. However, 'appropriately dressed' in any situation must be interpreted in its cultural context. At a social event such as a wedding reception, appropriate apparel for Western men may be a suit and tie but, at a traditional African wedding, they may appear to be inappropriately dressed.

artefacts

Artefacts are the personal items we wear or keep close to us and are another important aspect of physical appearance. Your jewellery, cars, watches and make-up all communicate a message about who you are and your status or position in society. In the work context, it has been suggested that jewellery should be kept to a minimum until you have established what is considered appropriate in your particular organisation.

2.3.6 Paralanguage

paralanguage

The vocal signs that accompany spoken language are termed *paralanguage*. It is concerned with the **sound** of the voice and the range of meanings that people convey through their voices rather than the words they use. The two main categories of paralanguage are vocal characteristics and vocal interferences.

vocal characteristics

Vocal characteristics are the pitch (the highness or lowness of your voice), volume (how loudly or softly you speak), rate (the speed at which you speak) and quality of the voice (how pleasant or unpleasant your voice sounds). Each characteristic influences the impression others have of you. For example, a loud voice is often associated with aggressiveness; people who speak quickly are said to be nervous.

vocal interferences

Vocal interferences are the sounds and words we use when we hesitate or are not sure of the right word. We all use the occasional 'uh', 'er', 'well', and 'you know' to indicate that we are searching for the right word. But such interferences become a problem when they are excessive and interrupt your listeners' concentration and comprehension.

2.4 Nonverbal skills

The greatest problem about nonverbal communication is that most of us don't pay sufficient attention to our own and other people's use of it. The best way to improve your understanding of the nonverbal cues you receive from others is to make a conscious effort to interpret both their verbal and nonverbal communication — what they say and how they say it. We emphasise again that nonverbal messages cannot be viewed as fixed and unchanging — they are influenced by context and culture. People who ascribe rigid meanings to nonverbal signs are prone to stereotyping. They allow their personal biases and feelings to influence their communication encounters. In the same way that different people ascribe different meanings to words on the basis of their attitudes, background, feelings and beliefs, so too do they attach different meanings to nonverbal cues.

The best way to improve your own nonverbal communication — the way you send messages without the use of words — is to consider the effects created by each of the categories we have discussed and to relate them to your own behaviour. The following four techniques may help.

1   Pay careful attention to the feedback you get from others. If you find that people regularly misunderstand your meanings and feelings, it could be that your verbal and nonverbal messages are incongruous (that is, they do not convey the same meaning). Use their feedback to try to improve your nonverbal communication.

2 Ask your friends and family to tell you about any distracting mannerisms of which you may not be aware and make a conscious effort to avoid them. People often do not know that they are playing with a strand of hair, swinging their feet or saying 'OK' or 'Well, you know ...' too often.

3 Observe the nonverbal communication of others. If you find some of their nonverbal behaviour irritating or distracting, make sure that you are not doing the same things!

4 Try to record yourself on audiotape or videotape, and study the results critically to identify some of the nonverbal habits of which you may not be aware. You can then work on improving aspects such as the tone of your voice, posture, appearance or hand gestures.

Case 2.1
Study the constitutional pamphlet on the next page, paying particular attention to the drawings which include people, and then make notes of which of the six categories of nonverbal communication are represented in the drawings.

Summary

In this unit we have established that communication is not merely a matter of exchanging verbal messages. People also use a large number of cues or signs to send messages to one another. We discussed the following functions of nonverbal communication: to reinforce, complement, contradict, replace or regulate a verbal message. We then emphasised that there is no 'recipe' for understanding nonverbal communication. It is influenced by factors such as context and culture and is often beyond our control. We continued with a discussion of the following categories of nonverbal behaviour: kinesics, proxemics, haptics, chronemics, personal appearance and paralanguage. We provided some hints for improving our nonverbal skills in everyday communication and ended the unit with a case study based on a constitutional pamphlet.

Case 2.1

This case consists of a pamphlet which was issued prior to the adoption of The Constitution of the Republic of South Africa (Act 108 of 1996). The pamphlet was designed to answer the sort of questions people were asking about the Constitution, especially with regard to how it was going to affect their lives. We reproduce the pamphlet below.

Your guarantee for a better South Africa

The new Constitution has taken months of negotiation. It is a very important document that is going to affect all our lives. Many people are asking all kinds of questions about it. This pamphlet is there to answer some of them. We hope it answers yours too.

THE NEW CONSTITUTION IS THE SET OF RULES ON WHICH THE COUNTRY WILL RUN

I keep hearing about the new Constitution, but I don't understand it. What is it all about?
It's not so complicated, really. A Constitution sets out the basic rules of a country. Everybody has to obey them — the President, Parliament, every man and woman.

What's so special about the new Constitution?
It says everyone is equal, black and white, whatever language you speak, whatever part of the country you come from.

What have the elections to do with the Constitution?
The Constitution says that every permanent resident in

South Africa, who is 18 years or over, shall have the right to vote. The more votes a party gets, the more seats it will have in Parliament.

What will happen to the present Parliament?
It will be completely replaced by the new one.

And the government?
It will also be new. The National Assembly will choose the President and Deputy Presidents.

And all the Cabinet Ministers? The Minister of Law and Order, or Education?
The President will have to choose Cabinet Ministers from all parties in Parliament. The more support

these parties have, the more ministers they will have.

Is that what they mean by a Government of National Unity?
Exactly. For five years all the parties, except the very tiny ones, will be entitled to a place in government.

Maybe my home language is the one I not only prefer to speak, but the one I'd like my children to read and write in. How is that going to be possible now?
Very easily — because this is such a basic right that it's one of the strong points of the Constitution now. All South African languages will be official — that means they'll be spoken, taught and communicated.

If I want to protest against something will I be able to march or speak my mind?
Under the new Constitution everyone has the right to assemble and demonstrate peacefully. Your fundamental rights cover things like free

speech, political rights, trade union rights etc.

What recourse do I have if any of my rights aren't respected?

You use the law — the Constitutional Court, after April 27th 1994, will make sure your fundamental rights are protected and respected.

What about land or ownership and the rights that govern them?
Everyone will have the equal right to own property according to the new Constitution. Even the people who lost their land or property will be attended to.

Who will make the laws?
The National Parliament will make laws about issues that affect the whole country. Each Province will also have its own Provincial Parliament which will pass laws dealing with matters that affect the Provinces.

What matters are these?
Take health. The National Government will deal with the overall health programme for the country and the qualifications of doctors and nurses. The Provincial Government will deal with health promotion in the province, where hospitals and clinics should be located, who should be appointed to staff them, etc.

I keep hearing that the elections are going to be "free and fair" — but I want to know who checks where my vote is going?
It's not possible for anyone to check.

Does anyone see my name during voting?
No — it works like this — after you've shown your ID or voter's card, you go to vote in secret.

Why must I have my ID or voter's card?
Just to allow you to vote as a permanent resident of this country. It's got nothing to do with the actual voting procedure — that's your private

concern and nobody need ever know — except if you decide to tell them.

What's going to happen to the defence and police forces?
There'll be a new defence force and a new police force that work for a new nation. They'll both be there to serve the community.

Is there really going to be no discrimination whatsoever?
Discrimination has become a rather dirty word and you'll be able to use the law to protect you against any of it — whether it be linguistic discrimination, religious or cultural.

Lots of people haven't been able to be educated before. What will happen now?
Now everyone will have the right to a basic education and equal access to that education. And wherever reasonably practical, you'll have it in the language of your choice.

Are women's rights going to be protected?
Of course — the new Constitution even provides for establishing a Commission on Gender Equality. Just to ensure women are respected and their rights protected.

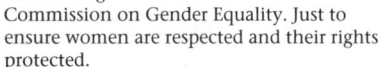

What can we expect South Africa to look like — and how will it operate according to the Constitution?
There'll be 9 new provinces and each one will have it's own Constitution so it'll be quite different. The provinces will govern themselves and make their own laws on issues such as agriculture, own language policy, education except universities and technikons, housing, health policy and welfare.

When do all these things come into effect?
On the 27th April 1994. After that, no government will be able to pass laws that conflict with our Constitution.

You have the right to know. In the interest of democracy the Transitional Executive Council wants you to be an informed voter.
Published by the TEC, Private Bag 878, Pretoria 0001.

OUR NEW CONSTITUTION

Source: National Archives of South Africa

Test-yourself

1 Define the five functions of nonverbal communication. Illustrate your answer with examples from your everyday experience of communication.

2 Describe the relationship between verbal and nonverbal communication.

3 Briefly explain the meaning of the following categories of nonverbal communication and illustrate each with an example from your own experience: kinesics, proxemics, haptics, chronemics, personal appearance and paralanguage. Do not write more than 10 lines for each category.

4 Study figure 2.4 below and list the nonverbal codes that are represented.

Figure 2.4: Nonverbal communication I

5 Study Figure 2.5 on the opposite page and suggest what differences in meaning the raised fist would have for the two men in the foreground and the uniformed man in the background.

Figure 2.5: Nonverbal communication II

Suggested reading

Birdwhistell, RL. 1970. *Kinesics and context: essays on body motion communication.* Philadelphia: University of Pennsylvania Press.

Burgoon, JK, Boller, BB & Woodall, WG. 1989. *Nonverbal communication: the unspoken dialogue.* New York: Harper & Row.

DeVito, JA & Hecht, M. 1990. *The nonverbal communication reader.* Prospect Heights, Ill: Waveland.

Hall, ET. 1969. *The hidden dimension.* New York: Doubleday.

Hall, ET. 1973. *The silent language.* Garden City, NY: Anchor Books.

Knapp, ML. 1980. *Essentials of nonverbal communication.* New York: Holt, Rinehart & Winston.

Leathers, DG. 1991. *Successful nonverbal communication: principles and applications.* 2nd edition. New York: Macmillan.

Lustig, MW & Koester, J. 1993. *Intercultural competence: interpersonal communication across cultures.* New York: HarperCollins.

Malandra, L, Barker, L & Barker, D. 1989. *Nonverbal communication.* 2nd edition. New York: Random House.

Mehrabian, A. 1981. *Silent messages.* 2nd edition. Belmont, Calif: Wadsworth.

Intrapersonal communication

Overview

Tina stretched lazily as she woke one morning and thought, "Good, it's Saturday and I'm meeting Amos for lunch. I'm going to wear my new outfit — it makes me look even sexier than usual and I want to make a really good impression on him." She opened the curtains to check the weather and decided that, as it was overcast, she had better take an umbrella with her. "I don't want to ruin my new clothes." She joined her dad for a cup of coffee in the kitchen, but found it difficult to concentrate on what he was telling her because she was planning what she would say to Amos during their lunch date. She had heard from mutual friends that he had won a scholarship to an overseas university, and was concerned that she was not clever enough to talk to him about topics that would capture his interest.

In the first few moments of the day, Tina was already engaging in the mental activity of talking to herself, or intrapersonal communication. Her thoughts ranged from her appearance to her lunch date and the weather, to the conversation she was going to have with Amos. Although we are not always conscious of the fact that we are constantly engaged in *self-talk*, communication scholars have become increasingly aware of the important role that intrapersonal communication plays in the nature of our relationships. In this unit we discuss the most important ideas that have emerged from research into the intrapersonal communication context.

We begin by examining the concept *self* and its various parts: the private and public self as well the physical, emotional and intellectual self. Our communication with ourselves and others depends to a large extent on the way we perceive the world around us. We therefore discuss the process of perception and consider its influence on our understanding of ourselves and others. We first consider the way we perceive ourselves and develop a self-concept, and then look at the way we perceive other people and form impressions of them. Some of the intrapersonal variables that also play a role in how we see ourselves and others are briefly described. This is followed by a discussion of the relationship between intrapersonal communication and needs and then the relationship between intrapersonal communication and self-disclosure. We end the unit with a case which is based on the way perception influences our concept of ourselves.

Learning outcomes

At the end of this unit you should be able to do the following.

1   Describe the concept *self* and its various parts.

2   Explain the process of perception by referring to selection, organisation and interpretation.

3   Explain how one's self-concept develops.

4   Explain how the concept you have of yourself influences your communication with others.

5   List four factors that influence our perception of others.

6   Identify and give an example of each component of Maslow's hierarchy of needs.

7   Define *self-disclosure* and give examples of it in at least two of your relationships.

8   Identify the difference in your openness in two relationships that are important to you.

9   Apply what you have learned about intrapersonal communication to your everyday communication experiences.

10 Be more sensitive to your own and other people's feelings in interpersonal relationships.

11 Answer the questions based on the case at the end of this unit.

Introduction

intrapersonal communication

Because we are human, we are constantly involved in planning, dreaming, thinking and worrying about what is happening in the world around us. In other words, we are constantly engaged in **intrapersonal communication** — communication within the self to the self (Ellis & McClintock 1994). Research conducted into intrapersonal communication confirms the view that "The first step towards effective communication with others is successful communication with yourself" (Barker & Gaut 1996:111). But what is the *self* with which we communicate?

3.1   The self

the self

The concept **self** is used to describe who and what we think we are — that is, our personal identity. Stewart (1990:115) defines the self in two dimensions: the self is "an **internal** thing — a composite of personality characteristics, attitudes, values, beliefs and habits that make us unique". And it is also a **social** thing — "it grows out of contacts with others and functions primarily to guide our communication". Take note that the self and communication are closely related — the self is shaped in relationship with others and, in turn, the self guides our communication and relationships with others.

private self
inner self

public self
social self

Even before reading this, you might already have expressed a similar view about the two dimensions of the self by saying that you have a **private** self and a **public** self. The private or inner self is often at variance with the public or social self that we display to others. The complexity of modern society demands that we in fact display a variety of public selves, for example as friend, employee, bank clerk, spouse, parent, student or soccer goalie. The well-known theorist Erving Goffman (1975) maintains that we are constantly engaged in playing roles or staging performances in order to create the desired impression on other people. It is in internal conversation that we can discard the masks we wear in public and get to know the private self.

physical self

We are in fact many selves (Burton & Dimbleby 1995; Barker & Gaut 1996). One such self is the **physical** self — the material body with its internal functions and outward appearance. The number of advertisements for preparations that will make you lose weight, look more beautiful, build stronger muscles, or improve your resistance to disease is indicative of our awareness of the physical self. The physical self — the part that others see — is often referred to as the material self because many people identify themselves in terms of what they have — their material possessions, such as their car, house, clothes, and so on.

emotional self

Another self is the **emotional** self. Some people are regarded as more emotional than others because they respond 'from the heart' (emotionally) rather than 'with the brain' (rationally) to a variety of situations, especially those involving fear, tension or conflict. The **intellectual** self is

intellectual self

associated with our mental processes and has to do with problem-solving, reasoning, analysis and logical thinking. Reading this text is an attribute of the intellectual self.

There are two important features regarding the self of which we should be aware. Firstly, we cannot separate the parts of the self — in reality they all work together. We see ourselves as a whole and our communication reflects the whole self. Secondly, the self is not inborn or static, but rather active and dynamic. It grows and changes throughout our lives. You will recall that Tina's concept of her physical self is that she is sexy, while her concept of her intellectual self is that she might not be clever enough to hold Amos's interest. How did she form these impressions? To answer the question, we need to briefly examine the process of perception.

3.2 Perception

perception

Ellis and McClintock (1994:1) define **perception** very broadly as "information which is taken in by the senses, processed by the brain, stored in memory and produces some form of physical or mental response". Human beings are equipped with the five senses of hearing, sight, touch, taste and smell. We gain information about ourselves and the world we live in through the interaction of these senses with the environment. The first time you touched a hot stove, you reacted by instinctively withdrawing your hand (a physical response). The information that heat burns the skin was processed by your brain and stored in memory so that you would not repeat the action in future.

A feature of perception is that it is a personal process which provides each of us with a unique view of the world. It does not, however, always provide us with an **accurate** representation of the world. The result is that our understanding of many situations can be distorted. Some people distort the information that comes to them through their senses to such an extent that their perception of themselves, others, and the events around them have little resemblance to reality. The two major causes of perceptual distortions are perceptual inaccuracies and the element of subjectivity in the perception process.

3.2.1 Perceptual inaccuracies

To illustrate that our sense organs can create perceptual inaccuracies, look at the two figures below. Which appears longer?

Figure 3.1: The Müller-Lyer illusion

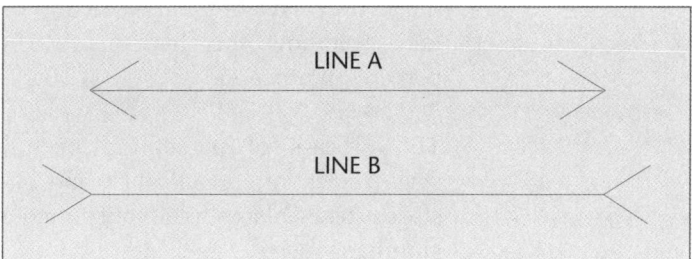

LINE A

LINE B

This is a well-known phenomenon called the Müller-Lyer illusion. If you've never seen the figure before, you would probably trust the evidence of your eyes that line B is longer than line A. Those who have seen it before will know that the two lines are the same length. Measure them to make sure!

A similar effect can be seen in figure 3.2.

Figure 3.2: Illusion of quantity related to space

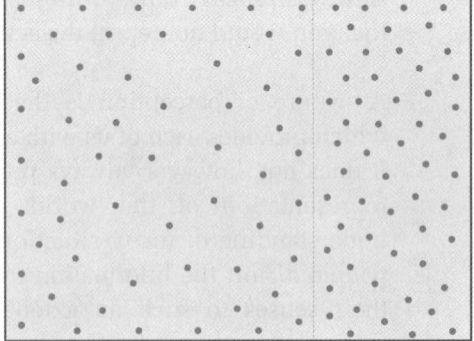

At first glance it looks as though there are more dots on the right side than on the left. In fact there are the same number on each side, but those on the right are packed into a smaller space.

3.2.2 The perception process

A second contributor to perceptual inaccuracies is the element of subjectivity in the process of perception. Perception is not merely a physical or mechanical act. People play an active role in the process. As a result, the image they have of themselves and others can be distorted. Let's see how this happens by briefly examining the perception process.

The process of perception occurs in three principal stages: selection, organisation and interpretation. The three stages take place relatively unconsciously and almost simultaneously.

selection

▶ **Selection:** We select only some aspects of information from the environment — those which attract our attention at a given time. When you are deeply engrossed in a book, for example, it is unlikely that you will hear the ticking of your alarm clock or the traffic noises in the background. It is only when your attention lapses that you pay attention to these sounds. This phenomenon is often explained by comparing the sense organs to receivers which are tuned to pick up all sorts of information, and the brain to the control mechanism which makes the information meaningful. The first stage in the perception process is that, from the variety of information your senses receive, your brain selects that which is relevant in a particular situation.

organisation

▶ **Organisation:** Once the brain has selected the relevant material, it arranges its selections into a meaningful whole. Look at the shapes in figure 3.3. You probably had no difficulty in identifying the shapes because your mind unconsciously completed or closed the incomplete shapes to provide you with a whole image.

Figure 3.3: Perceptual closure

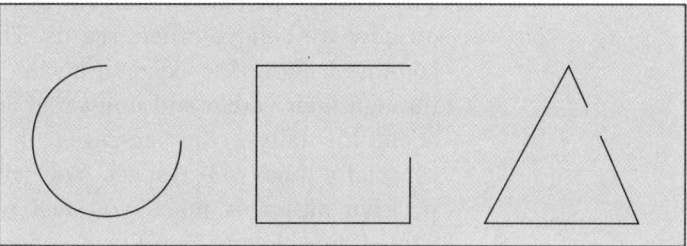

interpretation

▶ **Interpretation:** After sensory stimuli have selected and organised, we give meaning in light of our frame of reference (our personal circumstances and past experiences) in what is called perceptual interpretation. Because people are individuals, they are unlikely to select the same sensory information or to organise it in the same way. They are thus unlikely to arrive at the same interpretation of events or other people. The example is often given of three bystanders who witness the same road accident, yet provide three different accounts of the sequence of events that led to the accident. All three saw the same events, but interpreted them in terms of the information they had selected and organised.

INTRAPERSONAL COMMUNICATION **73**

Bearing in mind that perception is not always accurate, we now consider the relationship between intrapersonal communication and self-concept.

3.3 Intrapersonal communication and self-concept

self-concept

The way in which people perceive themselves creates the mental image or *self-concept* they have of themselves (self-image and self-esteem are synonymous terms). That image often differs from the concept others have of them. Self-concept can be described as everything that people think and feel about themselves. It includes appearance, physical and mental capabilities, attitudes and beliefs, strengths and weaknesses — that is, it includes the whole self. It is this mental image that is communicated to others through the way you behave in a particular situation (Verderber 1990).

How does self-concept develop? We said earlier that our self-concept is shaped by our relationships with others. The way we perceive ourselves depends to a large extent on how we believe others see us. The link with others is communication. We become aware of how others see us through their verbal and nonverbal communication. Think about the effects the messages of others have on you, especially those you respect. You will probably agree that positive messages make you feel accepted, worthwhile, valued, lovable and significant, whereas negative messages tend to make you feel inferior, worthless, left out, unloved or insignificant. In general, the more positive you feel about factors such as your physical appearance, capabilities, and the impression others have of you, the more positive your self-concept and your communication about yourself. The more negative you feel about yourself and the impression others have of you, the more negative your self-concept and the way you communicate about yourself.

Messages do not have to be overtly positive or negative to have an effect on you. Think back to what we said about the content level and relational level of messages in unit 1. Assume that you ask me how I am feeling today, and I say "Fine, thanks". On the content level, I offer some information.

At the same time, I also convey a relational message. If I smile as I answer, I tell you that I am happy to continue the conversation. If I respond sharply, then I imply that you are bothering me and I don't want to continue the conversation. In both cases the content is similar but the relational information differs. If you constantly receive negative relational messages, the way you see yourself will be undermined. On the other hand, frequent positive relational messages will reinforce your self-concept.

From a communicological point of view, the concept you have as an adult is the outcome of perceptions that have been provided by your parents, teachers, friends and others since birth. If you think about the process of perception we discussed earlier, you can understand why the image you have of yourself can be distorted. The element of subjectivity in interpreting sensory information can result in an inaccurate perception of yourself. A problem is that such inaccuracies often cause self-fulfilling prophecies.

3.3.1   Self-fulfilling prophecies

self-fulfilling prophecies

Self-fulfilling prophecies occur when our expectations of an event help to create the very conditions that allow the event to happen. Self-fulfilling prophecies colour your self-concept. For instance, a child who achieves success in the early grades at school will develop a better self-concept than the child who experiences constant academic failure. However, the potentially successful child who is constantly criticised by the teacher and told that he or she will never amount to much, often behaves in precisely the way the teacher predicted. The teacher's remarks contribute to his or her poor self-concept and, as a result, he or she is often inattentive and performs below his or her potential ability.

Self-fulfilling prophecies are usually carried over into adulthood. A child who is constantly criticised at home and made to feel worthless may develop a poor self-concept without being aware of the reason behind it, and often feels worthless as an adult. On the other hand, the child whose parents constantly tell him or her how brave and clever he or she is, is likely to grow up with an image of himself or herself as brave and clever. As an adult, he or she may well become an entrepreneur who is not afraid to take risks in his or her business and is willing to try out new courses of action. Thus childhood or teenage experiences influence adult interpersonal relationships.

3.3.2 Improving self-concept

Most of us would like to improve the image we have of ourselves. However, too often people decide they are going to change their behaviour overnight and are then disappointed when they fail. Change is a gradual process and requires a great deal of self-discipline. It is helpful to set realistic goals for yourself and encourage someone close to you to monitor your efforts. Pick one area in which you would like to improve yourself and see if you can work out why you have had problems in this area. Are you perhaps living out a self-fulfilling prophecy?

Try to deliberately become aware of your communication behaviour to determine how it has been influenced by other people's messages. Do the people in your environment support you in your endeavours or do they deliberately try to hold you back? Has someone else defined the roles you play? For instance, many husbands attempt to control the way their wives behave as spouses or parents. Such situations often lead to poor interpersonal relationships. Can you change such circumstances so that you are in control?

Learn to monitor the positive and negative feedback that others send you and adjust your behaviour accordingly. Some individuals who were raised by overly critical parents, for example, find it difficult to accept the positive comments about themselves they receive from others. Others simply choose to ignore the negative feedback they receive.

It is important to be aware of how accurately you perceive the context in which you are communicating. You may regard yourself as a humorist because people usually laugh at your jokes. When you are being interviewed for a job, however, you are expected to answer certain questions carefully rather than relate anecdotes that would go down well at a party.

3.4 Perception of others

How do we form perceptions of others? The interaction between the senses and the environment also provides us with information about the people with whom we come into contact. You are introduced to Peter at a conference, for example, and would like to find out which company he represents. Before you even start a conversation, you form an impression of him. This impression influences your reactions to him and determines what you will say and how you will say it. If you perceive him as arrogant and self-centred, your communication will be different than if you perceive him as friendly and outgoing. It is difficult to explain how such impressions are formed, but they are certainly related to your perception of him. His nonverbal communication — his tone of voice or the manner in which he shook your hand — could have created the impression; perhaps his clothing or his posture contributed to the impression. Your interpretation of the information about Peter that your brain selected and processed has been influenced by your past experiences of people, and creates your perception of Peter. The problem is that we tend to take our perceptions for granted without considering whether they are correct. At times our impressions are so inaccurate that our understanding of people and situations is distorted. An awareness of how inaccuracies in our perception of others occur can help to improve our relationships.

3.4.1 Perceptual inaccuracies of others

emotional state

▶ **Emotional state:** The feelings people experience at a particular time affect the nature of perception. First impressions are especially vulnerable to fluctuations in mood. When you are feeling low or irritable, your perception of others is generally more negative than if you are having a good day. Think about how your feelings may have affected your perception before acting on first impressions.

selective perception

▶ *Selective perception:* Selective perception refers to the fact that people choose information according to their existing attitudes, values and beliefs. Briefly, it means that people see what they want to see and hear what they want to hear. For instance, you tend to think highly of a person you like, and perceive only the positive side of her personality. The negative traits of that person, which may be apparent to other people, are often overlooked or ignored.

halo effect

▶ *Halo effect:* The halo effect occurs when we form perceptions of people based on the observation of a single characteristic which they display. We allow that characteristic to influence our impressions of that person without first verifying them. In an experiment described by Tubbs and Moss (1991), half the students in an economics class at the Melbourne Institute of Technology were given a note in which they were told that their new lecturer was considered to be a rather **warm person**, industrious, critical, practical and deter-mined. The other half were given a note which told them that he was considered to be a rather **cold** person, industrious, critical, practical and determined. After the lecturer had finished speaking, the students were asked to rate him on fifteen different characteristics. Those who were given the 'warm' note usually described the lecturer as social, popular and informal. Those who read the 'cold' description felt he was formal and self-centred. It appears that a halo effect can work to a person's advantage or disadvantage, depending on whether the perception is favourable or unfavourable.

stereotypes preformed judgements of people

▶ *Stereotyping:* As we form impressions of other people, we tend to classify them into categories on the basis of their characteristics. We put them into groups based on their race, religion, occupation, age, gender, physcial disabilities, accent or socio-economic level. Thus we think about a teenager, a foreigner, a lawyer, a trouble-maker or the elderly and assume that they will display all the characteristics we have come to associate with that type. Furthermore, the way we communicate with them will be based on the way we expect them to behave, rather than responding to each person as an individual.

3.4.2 Improving the accuracy of your perceptions

Improving the accuracy of your perceptions of others is largely a process of being mentally aware that one's initial perceptions are not always correct and that they may need to be revised. Verderber (1990) provides guidelines for constructing a more realistic impression of others and for assessing the validity of one's own perceptions.

▶ **Actively question the accuracy of your perceptions.** Many people act on their perceptions as though they were reality, saying 'I know what I saw'. Recognising the possibility of error motivates one to seek further verification and avoids erroneous impressions.

▶ **Withhold judgement until you have more information to verify your perceptions.** Taking the trouble to gather more information about people one meets helps to determine whether the original perception is accurate.

▶ **Talk with the people with whom you are forming perceptions.** The best way to get information about people and to get to know them is to talk with them. Some perceptions may still be inaccurate, but the likelihood of accuracy is increased.

▶ **Realise that perceptions of people need to change over time.** People's attitudes and behaviour often change, and one's perceptions of them need to change accordingly. It may be easier to hang onto one's original perceptions, but communication based on outdated, inaccurate perceptions can be more costly than revising one's perceptions.

▶ **Check perceptions verbally.** To avoid drawing the wrong conclusions from other people's nonverbal behaviour, it is important to make a perception check, a verbal statement that reflects one's understanding of the meaning of other people's nonverbal cues. For example, your mother uses a sharp tone of voice when she gives you instructions about the chores she would like you to do while she is at work. You say, 'From the sound of your voice, I get the impression I have done something to annoy you. Have I?' The question is the perception check. She may well be annoyed with you, in which case the perception check may lead to a discussion and resolution of the problem. On the other hand, she may be concerned about an entirely different matter and have inadvertently created your perception of the situation. In this case, the perception check may avoid misunderstandings and future problems.

▶ **Empathise with others.** Empathising means that we evaluate our perceptions from the viewpoint of the other person. We try to understand the other's point of view, and try to see the world as they see it. In addition to arriving at a more accurate perception of someone, this skill also counteracts our tendency to see the world only from our own point of view (Burton & Dimbleby 1995).

Throughout this section we have emphasised that perception is a personal process: your perception of a person, object or event is different from the actual person, object or event. In other words, you are the major actor in the perception process. By recognising that you have biases and that you are not always open to the information around you, you can increase the probability that your perceptions will provide you with accurate information about the world around you and the people in it.

There are a number of other intrapersonal factors which also create biases in our interpretation of ourselves, others and the events around us. Barker and Gaut (1996:123) refer to these as the "intrapersonal variables" that influence communication. Amongst others, they include your personality traits, past experiences and the defence mechanisms you use to resolve conflicts and anxiety. For example, the experiences of someone who has recently been divorced will no doubt affect that person's communication on the subject of marriage. Similarly, some of us deal with our failures by repressing them — that is, keeping certain thoughts and feelings below the conscious level so that we do not have to think about them. Others deal with the same situation by attempting to justify their failures — a process known as rationalisation. Some of these variables assist communication, while others create barriers to communication by interfering in the transmission and interpretation of messages. There are so many intrapersonal variables that influence our communication that we cannot discuss them all. For the purpose of this introductory course, we have limited our discussion to values, attitudes, beliefs, opinions and prejudices.

3.5   Intrapersonal variables

values

▶ *Values:* Values are the moral and ethical judgements we make about things that are important to us. All of us develop a value system as we develop from childhood to adulthood. Values can be a source of conflict within us as well as a barrier between people who have opposing standards. For example, should you value both friendship and honesty, you would try, at all times, to remain loyal to your friends and to be as honest as possible. But, how would you resolve the inner conflict that arises when given the choice between telling the truth to a friend who has asked your opinion about something, and risking hurting that person? Think about what your answer to the question tells you about your value system.

attitudes

▶ *Attitudes:* Related to values are attitudes. An attitude is a learned reaction to a person or situation. It implies a positive or negative evaluation of someone or something. A person who believes that pornography is detrimental to society would have a negative attitude towards any magazine or film, for instance, that contains and promotes pornography. In our relationships, people come to expect a pattern of behaviour from us based on what they have learned about our attitudes. Should we behave differently, they might say that we are acting out of character, and they might also revise their opinion of our attitudes and values.

beliefs

▶ **Beliefs, opinions and prejudices:** A **belief** is anything that is accepted as true without a negative or positive judgement. For example, you might believe in life after death, but your belief does not involve a positive or negative judgement of that idea. However, should you say that, because you believe in life in after death, it would be in our best interests to prepare for a life hereafter, you would be voicing an **opinion** on the subject.

opinions

Some of our beliefs and opinions are based on preconceived ideas and not on our own experiences. Such beliefs and opinions are the basis of the stereotypes, or preformed judgements about a person, group or thing, that we discussed in section 3.4.1. When stereotypes become deeply entrenched, we refer to them as prejudices. **Prejudices** are extremely dangerous because they are very resistant to change and are accompanied by strong emotional reactions (Ellis & McClintock 1994). Think about people who have strong racial prejudices and the emotional reactions that this produces. While none of us is entirely free from prejudices, some are more harmful to our communication and relationships than others.

prejudices

3.6 Intrapersonal communication and needs

A question that arises in the study of intrapersonal communication concerns the reasons that motivate the self to communicate in the first place. It is generally agreed that we communicate with some purpose in mind and that the most important purpose for which we use communication is to satisfy a personal *need*. Theorists in many disciplines have established the idea that needs are the driving force behind human behaviour. **Needs** are requirements of life which range from the physical need for food and shelter to the need to be given recognition for one's achievements. Certain needs, such as the sense of worth one derives from success, are geared towards the satisfaction and

needs

development of the self, and provide a strong motivation for communication (Burton & Dimbleby 1995). Each of us has our own individual sets of needs that motivate our communication and our responses to messages. While not everyone's priorities are identical, our needs resemble one another's sufficiently for scholars to have developed theories that establish the relationship between needs and communication.

3.6.1 Maslow's hierarchy of needs

hierarchy
a system of persons or things arranged in a graded order

Maslow (1970), a well-known psychologist, distinguished five basic levels of need: survival, safety, social, esteem and self-actualisation, which are depicted as a pyramid in figure 3.4. Maslow maintains that needs have to be aroused and remain unsatisfied for them to motivate behaviour. As you study the hierarchy, think about how each of the needs motivates your own communication behaviour (Wilson, Hantz & Hanna 1989; Kreps 1990; Bredenkamp 1996).

Figure 3.4: Maslow's hierarchy of needs

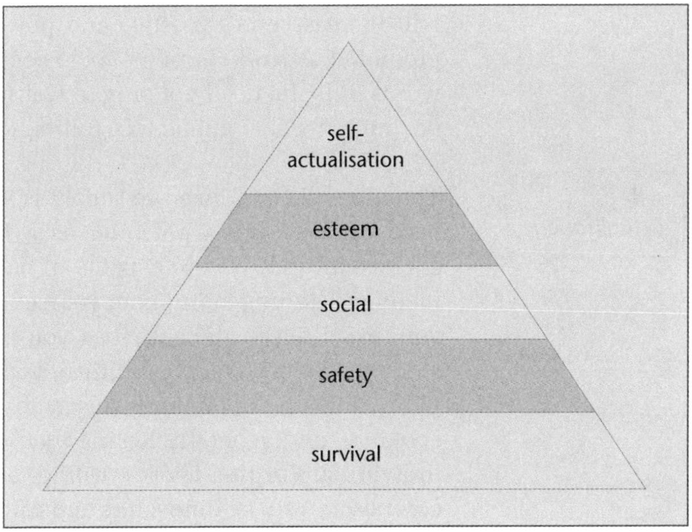

survival

Maslow contends that the most basic of all needs is the physical well-being or **survival** of the individual. Our physiological needs include the need for air, food, water, sleep and reproduction of the species.

safety

Safety or security needs are the next level of needs in the hierarchy. We need to feel secure and free from danger. We also have a need for structure, predictability, and law and order in our lives. Such needs are fulfilled by having shelter, a job, and feeling protected against bodily harm. For example, rising crime rates in our neighbourhood may lead us to instal a burglar alarm system in our homes.

social

The third level of needs, the **social** need, is the need to develop meaningful relationships with others. This category is related to the need to be accepted by others, to have friends, to belong to a group, and to be appreciated and loved by others. Social needs usually remain dominant until they have been satisfied, for instance in marriage, in close relationships with friends, or by joining a sports club or trade union.

esteem

The fourth level of needs, the **esteem** need, is the need to respect oneself and be respected by others. Enhancing one's self-respect or self-image may lead to activities such as private study or practice in a sport or skill, where needs pertaining to the regard of others lead to activities which will increase one's prestige and power, for instance being promoted at work, or one's socio-economic status. In other words, it is the need not only to feel successful in what you do, but to receive public recognition for your efforts.

self-actualisation

The most difficult need to satisfy is **self-actualisation**, the need to fulfil one's potential as a human being, and to achieve all that we are capable of being. Self-actualisation includes learning more about yourself and the world around you, excelling in the activities you perform (such as your studies or work responsibilities), becoming more satisfied with yourself, expressing your creativity (whether in art or cooking), and generally feeling that you are growing as an individual. On this level, we find, among others, writers, composers, artists, innovators and campaign leaders.

Maslow contends that these needs follow a hierarchical order and that people have to satisfy lower-order needs such as hunger and thirst before higher-order needs become important. The importance they attach to particular messages reflects these needs. For example, Maslow would say that, when you are in physical danger, messages about safety usually take priority over others. However, if you were starving, you might decide to risk your physical safety to obtain food. The person who has been retrenched and is worried about how he is going to pay the rent (a safety need) is more concerned with finding a job than with the admiration of his friends (esteem need). According to Maslow, self-actualisation only becomes important to people who feel secure in the knowledge that they have gained the respect (esteem need) and companionship (social need) of family, friends and colleagues.

While the hierarchy illustrates how our inner needs motivate us to communicate with others, Maslow's views also have shortcomings. The most important shortcoming is that the hierarchy reflects the society and culture of which he was a part. People from other cultures do not always agree with the hierarchical order in which he has placed the needs. Also, as Burton and Dimbleby (1995) explain, Maslow's highest need in the hierarchy is the product of a Western, industrial, individualised culture where the highest value is placed on self-actualisation — being able to fulfil your personal physical and emotional needs and desires, and ultimately to achieve a sense of independence. But, as we in South Africa are well aware, some cultures place the highest value on qualities such as mutual cooperation or equal opportunity for all. In such cultures, self-actualisation may be achieved by repressing your personal needs and desires and attending to those of other people and the community.

3.7 Intrapersonal communication and self-disclosure

self-disclosure

Self-disclosure is defined as "revealing one's thinking, feelings, and beliefs to another" (Gibson & Hanna 1992: 129), that is, revealing information about the private self to other people. Research confirms that self-disclosure is essential to the growth of meaningful interpersonal relationships. It is in intrapersonal communication that we decide how much information about the private self we are willing to reveal to other people. Telling someone something about yourself that he already knows would be sharing or disclosing information, but would not be regarded as self-disclosure. To qualify as self-disclosure, the information must be something that is normally kept hidden from most people, such as your deepest feelings or intimate thoughts (DeVito 1989).

The importance of self-disclosure is that it encourages the building of relationships. We know from experience that the types of relationships we share vary in quality and intensity. Some are extremely rewarding, while others are casual and almost meaningless. All of us have relationships in which we reveal or self-disclose more about ourselves than in others. There are some topics we would not even think about discussing with particular people. There are some relationships in which we keep our thoughts and feelings to ourselves, and others in which we are sufficiently comfortable to allow people access to our most intimate thoughts and feelings.

Self-disclosure depends on a variety of factors. People with a positive self-concept are more likely to disclose information about themselves than those with a negative self-concept. People of status are usually unwilling to reveal information about themselves to people of lesser status. Generally, men are less inclined to make self-disclosures than women. And the values of one's culture also play a part. Some cultures firmly discourage conversation about one's intimate feelings and personal beliefs. However, research has shown that some degree of self-disclosure not only benefits relationships, but leads to a greater degree of self-esteem (Burton & Dimbleby 1995).

3.7.1 A model of self-disclosure

A model that helps us to assess the amount of information we disclose is the Johari window (see figure 3.5). The window is divided into four panes or quadrants. The panes represent four areas of the self which are defined in terms of what the person does and does not know about themselves, and in terms of what others do or do not know about that person.

Figure 3.5: The Johari window

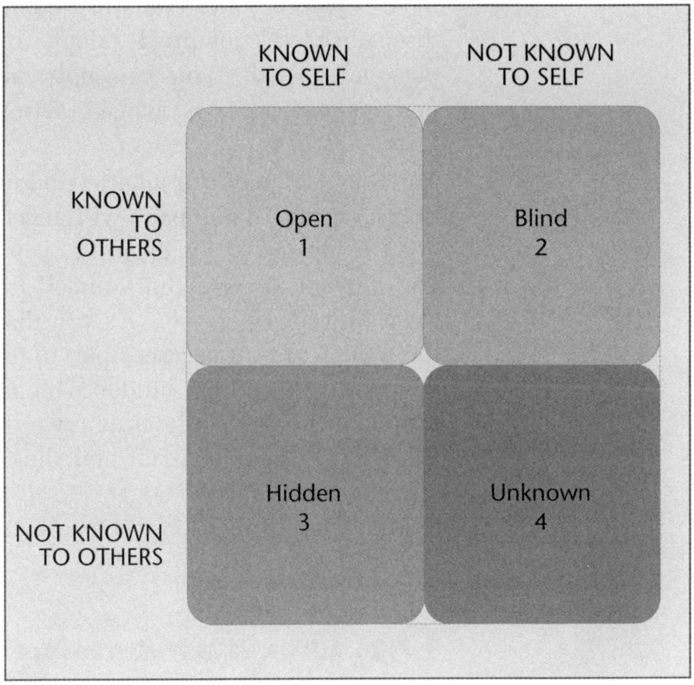

	KNOWN TO SELF	NOT KNOWN TO SELF
KNOWN TO OTHERS	Open 1	Blind 2
NOT KNOWN TO OTHERS	Hidden 3	Unknown 4

open pane

hidden pane

The **open pane** is the most public area and reflects your openness to the world and your willingness to be known. It comprises all aspects of yourself that are known to you and to others such as your name, your job or a club to which you belong. The **hidden pane** contains all the information you know about yourself that you prefer not to disclose to someone else. This area may include information about your salary, your marital problems, your failures and successes, your secret fears, and so on.

blind pane

unknown pane

The other two panes are areas where you don't know yourself. The **blind pane** represents all the things that others know about you, but about which you are not aware. This may vary from the way you twitch your nose during conversation to the way you tend to monopolise a conversation, react aggressively when people do not agree with your views, or you may be unaware of the high regard colleagues in your organisation have for the work you do. The **unknown pane** is the mystery area, known to no one. Burton and Dimbleby (1995) explain that it represents information about yourself which neither you nor others have explored. It contains qualities waiting to be discovered — untapped talents or your potential for personal growth. You can only **infer** that it exists or perhaps **confirm** its existence in retrospect.

The four panes of the Johari window are interdependent, thus a change in one pane will affect the others. If you are open to feedback, for example, you may discover things you did not know about yourself from others, and move them into the open area. As you disclose something from the hidden area, it becomes part of the open area; the open pane enlarges and the hidden pane is reduced. Luft (1970) proposes that not only is it rewarding and satisfying to learn more about yourself and thus gain self-insight, but also to reveal enough about yourself to enable others to get to know you better. Self-disclosure, however, also carries a degree of risk.

3.7.2   Risks of self-disclosure

Sometimes, disclosing too much of yourself to others early in a relationship may be inappropriate and costly — they may learn something about you that may stop the relationship from developing or cause it to deteriorate. Even in well-established relationships, inappropriate disclosures may have negative consequences. An admission of infidelity, for example, can cause a marriage to dissolve. The admission that you lost a job because you were accused of pilfering may cause people to reject you. According to the language theorist, Neil Postman, there is no good reason for people always to be totally honest if the relationship is going to suffer. He believes that our personal experience teaches us that "the capacity of words to exacerbate, wound and destroy is at least as great as their capacity to clarify, heal and organize" (Postman 1990:232). The point Postman is emphasising is that self-disclosure can be a two-edged sword. In some circumstances, it helps; in others, it defeats.

3.7.3 Self-disclosure guidelines

In the face of the contradictions presented between self-disclosing and withholding personal information, how are we to know how much about ourselves to reveal in a relationship? The consensus of opinion is that we have to take some risks if relationships are to grow. However, research results suggest that self-disclosure should only occur in relationships that are important to you.

Stewart (1990), for example, maintains that, while we choose to self-disclose because it will help others to know us, we should base our choices on a clear understanding of what is desirable and beneficial for the **relationship**. In other words, effective self-disclosure is disclosure that is **appropriate** to the situation and to the relationship between the people communicating.

DeVito (1989) and Verderber (1990) suggest that, because of the element of risk, disclosure in a relationship should occur gradually. We should not confide intimate details about ourselves immediately upon meeting someone — information about our sex lives or financial situation or political views, for instance. Rather, self-disclosure is the kind of communication that is revealed a little at a time as we come to trust the other person. By self-disclosing, we are in effect saying to others that we trust them, that we respect them, and that we would like the relationship to develop. Thus, a successful relationship is often marked by a balance of disclosure and feedback (disclosure from the other); that is, self-disclosure is reciprocal. This idea is explained by Myers and Myers (1992) in the following way:

> a relationship develops only when you and the other person are willing to go through the mutual process of revealing yourself to each other. If you can't reveal yourself, then you can not be close. To be silent about yourself is to remain a stranger (Myers & Myers 1992:211).

Case 3.1

(This case is adapted from Burton and Dimbleby 1995.)

Lerato was sitting in the cafeteria at work, drinking a cup of coffee and wondering why she had not got the promotion she had applied for. She was both disappointed and surprised because she had been so confident that by next month she would be a supervisor in her department. She had already planned on moving to a new flat because the increase in salary would have covered the higher rent. When Peter sat down next to her, she mumbled a greeting and hardly smiled at him. In reply to his question about what was bothering her, she started telling him about the interview with the management committee.

When she had finished, Peter said: "You know, I'm a friend as well as a colleague, and that's why I'm going to tread on your toes and perhaps sound unkind. But maybe you should think again about how you come across — how other people see you."

"What do you mean? I made sure that I answered all their questions positively and emphasised my abilities and strong points — I even told them about the changes I would implement immediately."

"Yes, but maybe they thought you were just too dominating."

"Dominating! I'm not dominating. Anyway, how can you be a supervisor unless you can show that you are in control of every situation?"

"Being in control doesn't mean that you have to always get your own way. I've seen you badger people until they agree with you — and they often don't like it." Seeing the look of amazement on Lerato's face, Peter quickly said: "Don't get me wrong. I like you. But you really tend to overpower people who don't go along with how you want to do things. You don't give them the opportunity to put across their own ideas. You even have to be in charge of our entertainment committee. What I'm trying to tell you is that management might have turned you down if that is how you came across at the interview."

Lerato was silent for a while and then said, "Funny, isn't it? I don't see myself like that at all. I thought I was always positive and helpful — actually a reasonable sort of person. I know that I do not have as many qualifications as some people in our department, so I thought that coming across as strong and helpful would make management appreciate me. Strange how wrong you can be about yourself."

"I'm not saying you're wrong," said Peter. "I'm only saying that other people don't see you quite the way you do."

After you have studied this case and thought about the situation, write down your own views about how the case relates to what you have studied in this unit: for example, perception of self and others, Maslow's hierarchy of needs, the development of self-concept, and self-disclosure. Then suggest ways in which Lerato could create better relationships with both her work colleagues and her superiors.

Summary

In this unit, we have focused on the intrapersonal communication context and its relevance in our lives. We began by examining the concept *self* and its various parts: the private and public self as well the physical, emotional and intellectual self. We then went on to explain that our communication with ourselves and others depends to a large extent on the way we perceive the world around us. We discussed the process of perception and considered its influence on our understanding of ourselves and others. We first considered the way we perceive ourselves and develop a self-concept, and then looked at the way we perceive other people and form impressions of them. Some of the intrapersonal variables that also play a role in how we see ourselves and others were briefly described: values, attitudes, beliefs, opinions and prejudices. We then discussed the relationship between intrapersonal communication and needs and the relationship between intrapersonal communication and self-disclosure. Throughout the unit we provided some guidelines intended to improve our intrapersonal communication and the way we understand ourselves and others. The unit ended with a case study based on the influence of perception on the development of self-concept.

Test-yourself

1   Briefly explain the process of perception by referring to selection, organisation and interpretation.

2   Explain how one's self-concept develops. Then briefly explain how the concept you have of yourself influences your communication with others.

3   List four factors that influence our perception of others.

4   Write a brief definition of each need in Maslow's hierarchy and provide an example from your own experience of how communication has helped you to satisfy each need.

5   Define self-disclosure and give examples of it in at least two of your relationships.

6   Identify the difference in your openness in two relationships that are important to you.

Suggested reading

Allport, GW. 1958. *The nature of prejudice.* Garden City, NY: Doubleday.

Barker, LL & Gaut, DA. 1996. *Communication.* 7th edition. Boston: Allyn & Bacon.

Cook, M. 1971. *Interpersonal perception.* Baltimore: Penguin.

Goffman, I. 1975. *The presentation of self in everyday life.* Garden City, NY: Doubleday.

Hartley, P. 1993. *Interpersonal communication.* London: Routledge.

Luft, J. 1970. *Of human interaction.* Palo Alto, Calif: National Press.

Lustig, MW & Koester, J. 1993. *Intercultural competence: interpersonal communication across cultures.* New York: HarperCollins.

Myers, G & Myers, M. 1992. *The dynamics of human communication.* New York: McGraw-Hill.

Rogers, CR. 1990. *On becoming a person: a therapist's view of psychotherapy.* London: Constable.

Schneider, DJ, Hastorf, AH & Ellsworth, PC. 1979. *Person perception.* Reading, Mass: Addison-Wesley.

Interpersonal communication

Overview

We spend a great deal of our time interacting with other people — at home, at school, at work or in social situations. If you think back over the last few days, can you remember how many of your waking hours you spent completely alone? You probably spent some of your time talking to a friend, discussing an issue with a parent, or chatting to a sales assistant about a purchase you were making. Even when you were alone, you probably spent some of your time reading a magazine or watching television, and were hence involved in interaction with a mass communicator. This unit is concerned with face-to-face interaction between people. We are mostly concerned with one-to-one relationships since unit 5 deals with communication in small groups. While you study this unit, it is important to remember that everything you have learned about communication thus far is pertinent to interpersonal communication.

We examine communication between two people more closely by focusing on the relationships that we develop and maintain in our everyday lives. We begin by giving a brief discussion of Martin Buber's description of two types of communication relationships: *I-you* and *I-it* relationships, and the consequences of each for the life of the individual. We then go on to consider three factors that influence the development and nature of our interpersonal relationships. The first factor concerns our ability to listen attentively to others. The second factor concerns our interpersonal needs and is illustrated by the theories of Schutz and Homans. The third factor concerns the communication style we use in our relationships: passive, aggressive or assertive styles of behaviour. Throughout the unit we provide guidelines for improving your own interpersonal relationships. We end with a case study based on three styles of communication behaviour.

Learning outcomes

At the end of this unit you should be able to do the following.

1   Briefly describe the characteristics of *I-you* and *I-it* relationships.

2   Define the three interpersonal needs in Schutz's theory and give an example of how each one motivated you to communicate with another person.

3   Explain Homans's social-exchange theory and describe a relationship you have maintained because it provides you with greater need fulfilment than cost.

4   Define *nonassertive communication* and relate a personal experience to illustrate it.

5   Define *aggressive communication* and relate a personal experience to illustrate it.

6   Define *assertive communication* and relate a personal experience to illustrate it.

7   List and explain three guidelines for improving assertive behaviour.

8   Apply the knowledge about interpersonal relationships you learn in this unit to your personal communication experiences.

9   Be more sensitive to your own and other people's feelings in interpersonal relationships.

10   Answer the questions based on the case at the end of this unit.

Introduction

Sociologists have noted that, as modern society becomes increasingly technological and impersonal, people seem to place a greater value than ever on meaningful relationships in their everyday lives. Research results demonstrate that the most important contributor to personal happiness — outranking money, job and sex — is a close relationship with another person (DeVito 1989). Stewart (1990:7) goes as far as asserting that "the quality of your life is directly related to the quality of your communication", an idea which Satir (1972:30) strongly reinforces in the following words: "Once a human being has arrived on this earth, communication is the largest single factor determining what kinds of relationships he makes with others and what happens to him in the world about him."

Communication scientists make the point that a great deal of time is spent in teaching children to read and write, to pronounce words and to use them correctly. But, very little time at school, college or university is spent in teaching people how to communicate effectively (Pease & Garner 1989). Communication is the foundation for all our interpersonal relationships. Through communication we establish, develop and maintain relationships; and through communication we also withdraw from and terminate relationships. The link between communication, inter-personal relationships, and the quality of life is the theme underlying the work of the philosopher, Martin Buber.

4.1 Buber's theory of interpersonal relationships

Before we discuss Buber's theory, please take note that the references to 'he' and 'him' in the discussion are not intended to be sexist. In Buber's lifetime (1878–1965), it was common practice to use the masculine form of address to refer to both men and women. We have tried as far as possible to use the masculine when Buber refers to the communicator and the feminine when he talks about the recipient, but these gender references are interchangeable.

According to Buber (1964; 1970), the basis of human existence is that people are communicating beings. Each of us is always in the process of communicating with the world (our circumstances), thereby making sense of the situation in which we find ourselves (intrapersonal communication). Other people are part of our circumstances and we enter into relationships with them as well. In Buber's view, it is the nature of the relationships that people form that determines their **mode of existence**. To express this thought simply: the meaning that life holds for each of us arises from the type of relationships we create with other people.

mode of existence
quality of life

Buber describes two types of interpersonal relationships: *I-you relationships* and *I-it relationships*. The difference lies in the nature of the communication that takes place between the participants. To understand the difference between the two relationships, we have to explain the concepts *dialogue* and *monologue* in interpersonal communication. A **dialogue** is a conversation between two people in which both participants have the opportunity to express themselves and to interpret each other's messages. An exchange of thoughts, feelings and meaning takes place between them. In a **monologue**, the communicator is in a sense the only participant. He expresses his point of view without taking into account the needs of the recipient or giving her the opportunity to respond meaningfully. It is a one-sided conversation in which no exchange of meaning between the participants is possible. Buber maintains that the **attitude** and **intentions** of the partners differ in the two ways of communicating (Johannensen 1971; Jansen & Steinberg 1991).

dialogue

monologue

4.1.1   The I-you relationship

In the **I-you relationship** the partners approach each other with mutual respect, sincerity and honesty, and the intention to become subjectively involved in a reciprocal relationship. Buber says that the *I* (communicator) reaches out to the *you* (recipient) with his whole being and the *you* responds with her whole being. Although interested in being understood, the *I* does not attempt to impose his views on the *you*, or to bolster his own self-image by giving

I-you relationship

off false impressions. Each reveals the person that they really **are** and not the image of themselves they would like others to have. Each communicates their own feelings, thoughts and beliefs, and not opinions they have heard from others.

In addition to revealing himself as he is, the *I* also accepts the other as the unique individual that she is. He is present to the other in the sense that he listens attentively to what she wishes to express and tries to understand her point of view. Buber explains that, in such a relationship, a space opens up between people — he calls it the **interhuman domain** — and it is here that dialogue unfolds and 'you' and 'I' become 'we'. The *we* or dialogical relationship is based on intersubjectivity: that is, the participants acknowledge the differences between them while striving to come to an understanding of each other. Buber stresses that in the *we* relationship neither partner is taken over by the other. Although the *we* relationship is characterised by involvement, equally important in the relationship is the idea of distance — this means that even in the closest relationship both partners retain their individuality. In the interhuman domain both participants acknowledge the other as a unique individual and simultaneously reach a deeper understanding of themselves.

interhuman domain

4.1.2 The I-it relationship

I-it relationship

In contrast to the *I-you* relationship is the **I-it relationship**. The main difference between the two relationships is in the attitude and intentions of the *I* to the other. In the *I-it* relationship, the attitude of the *I* is that his partner in communication is not an equal subject in the relationship, but an **object** to be manipulated for personal gain. Although there are two participants, the *I-it* relationship is not a dialogical relationship because the distinguishing features of the *I-you* relationship are not present. The intention of the *I* is to persuade the other to his way of thinking without taking into account the views and needs of the other, as in dialogue. The communicator is conducting a monologue, a conversation in which only his point of view and needs are considered.

Words that Buber uses to characterise the *I-it* relationship are, amongst others: **self-centredness**, **pretence**, **domination**, **exploitation** and **manipulation**. This is not a relationship of mutual trust, openness, and reciprocity, but one in which the communicator **uses** the recipient to achieve his own ends. There is no understanding of one another because the *I-it* relationship does not include the option of **agreement to differ**, but that the recipient must always agree with the communicator's views.

Buber does not condemn the *I-it* relationship. He acknowledges that in order to survive in the modern world *I-it* relationships are unavoidable. What he emphasises, however, is that *I-it* should not be allowed to overtake one's life: *I-it* should always remain subordinate to *I-you*. This is because the two relationships indicate two modes of existence. The *I-you* relationship implies an ***authentic*** mode of existence, one in which each participant individually determines the person they become and the meaning that life holds for them. The *I-it* relationship implies an ***inauthentic*** mode of existence, one in which the individual allows him/herself to be determined by the will of others with whom they come into contact. Ultimately, however, the type of relationship and mode of existence that predominates in each person's life remains the choice and responsibility of the individuals themselves.

> *authentic/ inauthentic mode of existence*

In the rest of this unit, we move away from philosophical thoughts about communication and relationships to a consideration of some of the factors that play a role in establishing and maintaining interpersonal relationships.

While relationships sometimes develop because people are initially attracted to one another by physical and personality factors, we do not usually form close relationships immediately upon meeting someone; rather we grow into a relationship gradually by getting to know more about one another through our communication. As the relationship develops, we learn about the other person as well as our reasons for forming particular relationships.

No single characteristic or factor can describe the complexity of interpersonal relationships. Theorists have proposed a variety of factors that need to be taken into account in the study of interpersonal relationships. The three factors we have selected seem to us to be among the most important because they play a prominent role in influencing the nature and quality of our relationships: the degree to which people listen attentively to each other; the degree to which people are able to satisfy each other's interpersonal needs; and the degree of assertiveness with which they express feelings in their relationships.

4.2 Interpersonal communication and listening

Researchers report that one of the major limitations in establishing and maintaining relationships is the inability of the partners to listen efficiently. And it is not only in interpersonal communication that we need listening skills. We use the telephone, attend lectures and meetings, participate in arguments, give and receive instructions, listen to the news on the radio or television, and make decisions based on oral information (Gamble & Gamble 1987).

Studies show that, while we often spend as much as 75 per cent of our communication time in listening, most adults listen at no better than 25 per cent efficiency (DeVito 1989). Think about these percentages — it means that we often do not hear as much as 75 per cent of a message! The reason is probably because most of us take the ability to listen for granted and do not think about it as a skill that we must learn.

hearing

listening

Listening is often explained by distinguishing it from hearing. **Hearing** is a passive process. When sound waves vibrate against the eardrum and the brain registers these sounds, we hear. **Listening**, like all acts of perception, is a dynamic, active process involving both the communicator and the recipient. Listening occurs when the signals or sounds sent to the brain are processed and used — that is, when we attend to what is being said, select what is relevant, and then understand and interpret it for ourselves. (Refer back to unit 3 if you need to revise the process of perception.) Efficient listening also requires that we remember what has been conveyed to us and that we respond to the communicator.

The listening process becomes even more complex when we communicate with others rather than listen to the sounds of nature or to music. In order to listen effectively we have to pay attention both to what is said (the verbal or content level of the message) and to the manner in which it is conveyed (the nonverbal or relational level of the message). We have to listen to the words that are being spoken and, at the same time, 'listen' to the nonverbal cues that accompany the words. The reason is that the nonverbal part of the message carries the feelings and emotions of the speaker, and often 'says' more than the words that are used. Active, efficient listening therefore helps us to interpret messages and responses more accurately and thereby to gain a better understanding of the people with whom we come into contact. In fact, poor listening is one of the major causes of misunderstanding in both our personal and professional relationships. As you study the following sections, you should relate the new information you acquire to your own interpersonal relationships and to Buber's description of *I-you* and *I-it* relationships. Although our focus is primarily on two-people relationships, we also make reference to listening in group situations. You will recall that, in unit 1, we pointed out that the settings we use to describe communication are not mutually exclusive and the distinctions among them are not clear-cut.

4.2.1 Types of listening

Your degree of involvement in a given interaction and the amount of energy you expend in listening distinguishes active from passive listening. You work harder at listening to a friend sharing a problem than listening politely to your grandmother telling you how different things were when she was young. The following types of listening provide an idea of the range of different levels at which we listen.

enjoyment

▶ **Listening for enjoyment:** Listening for *enjoyment* occupies a good deal of our listening time — we listen to music, to our favourite television programme, or to a friend sharing an interesting titbit of gossip or telling a humorous story. At such times we may suspend our critical faculties, relax and enjoy the stimulation (DeVito 1989).

information

▶ **Comprehensive or discriminative listening:** Listening is one of the primary means of obtaining *information*. The more efficient our listening skills, the more accurate will be the information we gather. Naturally, we listen for different sorts of information. The student taking notes in a communication lecture or the worker receiving instructions about how to perform a new task is listening for information or listening discriminately. The business world also requires people to listen for information. The secretary listening to her supervisor's instructions, the customer listening to the salesperson's description of a new product, or the shipping clerk listening to an order to ship 100 containers to Cape Town, are all listening for information.

critical

▶ **Critical listening:** *Critical listening* is the type of listening you engage in when you suspect that the source of the information may be biased — for instance, listening to a friend telling you why your political beliefs are not sound. Critical listening requires the skills needed to analyse, evaluate and challenge the content of the information. The field of persuasion offers you the greatest opportunity to use critical listening skills. Advertisements, political slogans, as well as persuasive messages from friends and family should be critically analysed and evaluated before you act on them.

▶ **Conversational and reflective listening:** We use all the types of listening discussed so far in our interpersonal communication — in conversation with either one other person or in a group. We listen for enjoyment, for information or, at times, to evaluate the topic of the conversation. *Conversational listening* implies a

conversational

constant exchange between the roles of the participants. You and your partner are expected to concentrate on each other's messages and to provide appropriate feedback.

reflective/ empathic

In close relationships, you engage in a different type of conversational listening by showing affection, caring and warmth to your partner. This is called **reflective** or **empathic listening**. Sometimes the situation arises where, for example, a friend in distress may need to talk to someone and you provide the necessary support by listening. In this situation, you are not usually required to listen for information or to be critical, but to listen for **feelings**. And you know that some feelings are often expressed nonverbally rather than verbally. Sharing feelings, whether they are of sorrow or joy, enables people to cope with them better. You have probably noticed how your distress over an incident is lessened after you have 'poured your heart out' to an understanding listener. Similarly, feelings of joy are often increased when they are shared.

4.2.2   Inefficient listening behaviours

The problem in all types of listening is that some of our listening behaviour hampers our effectiveness as listeners. The following are some behaviours of which we may not be aware but which impede efficient listening.

fidgeting

Fidgeting while someone is talking shows impatience and tells the communicator that you are distracted or not interested in the conversation and this discourages him or her from continuing. Think about the nonverbal messages you are conveying to the speaker when you scratch your head, pull on your earlobe or swing your feet while he or she is talking.

concentration

Lack of concentration is a prime cause of inefficient listening. If you allow your mind to wander during a conversation and perhaps think about what you are going to do later on, you are unlikely to pick up the ideas that are being expressed or to remember them. You are also unlikely to provide your partner with the feedback that tells him or her that you are interested in what he or she is saying and that you are listening.

inaccuracy

Inaccurate listening means that you either pay too much attention to the communicator's ideas and forget to interpret the emotions that are being expressed, or that you pay too much attention to emotional messages and neglect the ideas that are being expressed. You should remember that every message has two parts: the ideas that are spoken and the emotions that are conveyed through body movements and tone of voice (Abrams 1986). (The exception is that in reflective listening we purposefully concentrate on feelings.)

As well as poor listening behaviour, we identify some barriers to listening that have an equally negative effect on our ability to listen efficiently.

4.2.3   Barriers to listening

The general term used to describe anything that interferes with the communication process is *noise* (refer back to unit 1). With respect to listening, noise refers not only to loud sounds, but to anything that distracts us from listening. We call such interferences *listening barriers*. They can be categorised as external barriers and internal barriers (Abrams 1986).

external barriers

External barriers to listening are distractions in the listening environment. They include background sounds such as doors slamming, telephones ringing or jack-hammering in the street outside. The activities of people nearby, interruptions from others, and physical discomfort such as an uncomfortable chair or a hall with poor acoustics are also external barriers to listening. If you have ever tried to pay attention to instructions while your head of department constantly stops speaking to answer the telephone, you will know the extent to which environ-mental barriers can affect attention and remembering.

We cannot place all the blame for inefficient listening on external barriers. Some of the difficulties we encounter

INTERPERSONAL COMMUNICATION   **103**

stem from within ourselves. Distractions in the listener's mind are the personal prejudices that we call internal barriers to listening.

internal barriers

Internal barriers are the physical and psychological conditions that we bring to the communication situation that may inhibit active listening. These include feelings such as anger, anxiety and fatigue, as well as personal prejudices about the communicator's appearance, status, style of speaking and subject matter. Our attitudes often have detrimental effects on our communication. If, for instance, you see yourself as cleverer than other people, with nothing to gain from listening to them, you have created a psychological barrier. Similarly, if you make judgements based on stereotypes — perhaps that a man wearing an earring is a dropout, or that a woman knows nothing about economics — you will evaluate them on the basis of preconceived ideas about their appearance instead of listening to them.

Other internal barriers that impede active listening include jumping to conclusions about what the communicator will say, the tendency to ignore topics that are regarded as difficult, and the listener's inability to understand some of the words and ideas expressed by the communicator (refer also to the discussion of noise in unit 1).

4.2.4   Developing efficient listening skills

Active listening seems difficult to people who have never tried it. Because so many of the problems associated with listening have negative consequences, you should make the effort to practise the techniques described below to listen more efficiently (Gamble & Gamble 1987; Hybels & Weaver 1989; Rensburg & Bredenkamp 1991).

focusing attention

▶ **Focus your attention.** The first step in learning to listen more efficiently is to consciously make the effort to overcome your poor listening behaviours as well as the external and internal barriers that may be impeding your listening ability. Being an effective listener requires that you put aside daydreams and distractions and focus your attention on what the communicator is saying. Remember that your feelings and attitudes are as much a drawback to effective listening as distracting sounds.

showing attentiveness

▶ **Show that you are listening.** It is important not only to pay attention to others, but to show active signs of *attentiveness*. You can achieve this by offering them both verbal and nonverbal cues. Verbal cues can be comments such as "I see" or "Go on", or "Tell me more". Nonverbal cues also show that you are listening, for example by maintaining eye contact, smiling, frowning or nodding. Such feedback encourages the other person to give you the details necessary for better understanding and lets them know that you are involved in the interaction. At the same time, it is important to suppress what you want to say until the communicator has finished talking and not to interrupt while they are still expressing themselves.

understanding ideas

▶ **Listen to understand ideas.** Since it is not possible to remember every word of a complex message, you should work toward identifying only those concepts that are most important — in other words, those ideas that comprise the main points of the person's message. Thus, when you listen to understand, you actively concentrate on identifying the key words and phrases that will help you to accurately summarise the concepts being discussed.

retaining information

▶ **Listen to retain information.** Listening to retain information also requires attention and concentration. Some of the methods that help retention include the following.

anticipating

Anticipate what is coming. For example, if the speaker says, "The following five points are important", prepare yourself to listen to and remember the five points.

forming associations

Form associations. Some people remember names, places and numbers by associating what was heard with something that is familiar, or by associating it with a visual image.

note-taking

Take notes. When messages are complex, and accurate retention of information is important, note-taking is probably the most reliable method to recall information. In other words, you paraphrase what has been said by writing down main ideas and points.

analysing/ evaluating

▶ **Listen to analyse and evaluate content.** Listening critically calls for even greater skill than identifying and remembering ideas. Try to establish the communicator's motives and credibility by challenging and questioning the ideas expressed. To evaluate the validity of a message and then accept or reject it involves the ability to separate fact from opinion, determine if an argument is based on logic or emotion, and detect ambiguities in the argument (Barker 1984). You also need to recognise your own biases and prejudices about the topic. Hybels and Weaver (1989:65) express evaluation as follows: "We must learn to *suspend judgement* — delay taking a position — until all the facts and other evidence are in, we have had a chance to test the facts in the marketplace of ideas, or they have been chewed over sufficiently for digestion."

reflecting

▶ **Listen reflectively.** The best way to listen reflectively is to try to understand what the other person is feeling **from their point of view** and reflect these feelings back with empathy. It requires that you put aside your own feelings and opinions and make the effort to recognise the emotions being expressed and to encourage the person to come to terms with their feelings. We do this by paraphrasing the communicator's statements and reinforcing those statements with nonverbal cues — eye contact, touching and facial expressions. The following is an example of a reflective listening response in which the listener paraphrases the speaker's words and feelings. Thandi is confiding in Sipho about her studies.

Sipho replies: "You keep telling me how well everything is going and how pleased you are that your assignments are up to date. But every time you bring up the subject of credit marks for examination entrance your tone changes and you sound less enthusiastic. Is something bothering you?"

It is important to remember that is not your task to judge the situation. You help the other person reach a solution without offering advice in the form of "You shouldn't feel that way" or "Why don't you look for another job?" or "You must tell her you won't tolerate such behaviour". These are poor responses because they do not help the other person to address the feelings that are the cause of the problem.

4.3 Interpersonal communication and needs

Theories that have been developed about interpersonal needs provide a way of understanding why we and others behave as we do in our relationships. They help us to gain a deeper knowledge of ourselves, our motivations for behaving in certain ways, and the manner in which we communicate. By understanding other people's needs and motivations, we are more likely to identify their communication priorities, learn how to attract and hold their attention, and express ourselves in ways that they understand. As the relationship between two people grows, and they learn more about the needs that motivate them, it becomes easier to express themselves in ways that the other will understand.

In unit 3 we discussed the inner needs that motivate us to communicate with reference to Maslow's hierarchy of needs. Two theories that deal specifically with needs that are satisfied in interpersonal relationships are Schutz's (1958) interpersonal needs theory and Homans's (1959) social-exchange theory.

4.3.1 Schutz's interpersonal needs theory

The major premise of Schutz's theory is that people need people. He contends that the drive to develop interpersonal relationships with others is to satisfy three basic human needs: inclusion, affection and control. We all have these needs in varying degrees and express them in different ways.

inclusion

▶ **Need for inclusion:** The need for inclusion reflects a desire for social contact. Schutz found that we need to be in the company of others and to establish and maintain a feeling of mutual interest with them. When the need for inclusion is met, we tend to feel accepted, understood and worthwhile. When this need is not met, we tend to feel lonely and unwanted.

We all differ in the amount of interaction with others that will satisfy this need. Schutz describes people who feel little need to be included in groups and tend to avoid interacting with others — insisting that they prefer to be left alone — as **undersocial**. **Oversocial** people, on the other hand, continually seek the companionship of others and tend to join and feel part of many groups. Schutz concludes that both types fear being ignored or left out, but the overt behaviours they display to compensate for their fears are different (Gamble & Gamble 1987; Trenholm 1991).

undersocial/ oversocial

In reality, most people do not belong to either of these extreme types. They are the **adaptable-social** people who are able to balance their needs for inclusion and privacy. Such people can sometimes be comfortable being alone, but at other times need and enjoy interacting with others. According to Schutz, relationships function best when people are able to achieve a balance between the need to be alone and to be with others.

adaptable- social

▶ **Need for affection:** Schutz found that we all need opportunities to show **affection** for others as well as to receive affection. This need is reflected in the development of emotionally close relationships in which affection is shown and expressed both verbally and nonverbally. Again, people express varying degrees of this need by displaying different behaviours.

affection

At one extreme are the **underpersonal** individuals who value privacy and seem to have little need for affection. They avoid close ties, keep their feelings to themselves, and even respond with hostility to whose who want to display affection. **Overpersonal** people, on the other hand, have a high need for close relationships with others. They tend to confide in all the people they meet,

underpersonal

overpersonal

express their feelings openly and freely, and expect others to respond in the same way. Between these extremes are the **personal** people who are able to express and receive affection when desirable, but can also maintain a distance when necessary. Schutz maintains that personal people seem to be able to handle both close and distant (casual) relationships more comfortably than the other two types.

personal

control

▶ **Need for control:** The need for **control** is the desire both to successfully manage and influence the events and people around you and, at other times, to allow others to establish that control. As with the other two interpersonal needs, there are differing degrees of this need and different ways of displaying it.

abdicrat

Schutz describes **abdicrats** as people with a strong need to be controlled. They regularly assume a submissive or subordinate role in a relationship. They prefer not to make decisions or accept responsibility, but abdicate all power to their partner in the relationship. At the other extreme are **autocrats** who dominate others and feel that they must always be in charge. In fact, they become anxious if they cannot control a relationship and make every decision. The **democrat** falls somewhere between the two extremes. Such people know when it is appropriate to control and are able to do so, but they can also be comfortable submitting to others when necessary. Schutz found that relationships function best when the participants have a democratic relationship in which they share power easily and comfortably.

autocrat

democrat

We can conclude from Schutz's theory that understanding our own as well as other people's needs for inclusion, affection and control can go a long way to contributing to the success of our relationships. If you have a high need for affection, for instance, you are soon going to become frustrated in a relationship with someone who prefers not to reveal feelings openly or who dislikes being touched. On the other hand, if you are the sort of person who prefers not to shoulder responsibility, but your partner is happy to do so, the matter of control in your relationship should not create a problem. We can also understand why Schutz maintains that the most successful relationships develop between people who are not extreme in their interpersonal needs.

Schutz's theory contributes to our understanding of our interpersonal needs and helps us to make sense of our relationships. A theory that focuses on **why** we maintain some relationships and terminate others is Homan's social-exchange theory.

4.3.2 Homans's social-exchange theory

According to Homans (1959), all social interactions involve some sort of exchange or barter. For example, we may offer someone help in exchange for gratitude, talk in exchange for friendship, or love in exchange for security. In other words, we exchange one interpersonal need for another. In making this kind of bargain, we tend to calculate the rewards we are likely to receive and the costs we will incur on our investment. Homans maintains that, just as people pay for goods and services, they calculate the profits and losses in a relationship, and decide either to pursue or terminate it (Trenholm 1991).

reward

In terms of Homans's theory, a **reward** or profit is any positive outcome resulting from a relationship. Rewards are basically the things that fulfil our needs for security, social contact, sex, financial gain, status and so forth. Rewards, however, always involve some cost or payback. For example, in order to acquire the reward of promotion at work (financial gain and status), you might have to give up some degree of freedom. The payback for the promotion could be that your social activities are curtailed and your relationships with others consequently deteriorate. Or, you might find that it is not possible to maintain a friendship which provides you with satisfaction or rewards because your boyfriend does not get on with your friend. The cost of maintaining one relationship might be that you have to give up the other.

cost

In the same way, we calculate the **costs** incurred in maintaining our relationships and tend to terminate those which have a negative outcome: they create unhappiness, dissatisfaction and problems rather than happiness, satisfaction and pleasure. Social-exchange theory implies that we will work to maintain a relationship only as long as the rewards or profits we perceive for ourselves are greater than the costs. According to this theory, no interpersonal relationship continues for very long unless both parties think they are making a profit.

While this economic orientation may be too rational to explain interpersonal relationships fully, it nevertheless adds to our knowledge by putting into clearer perspective the human tendency to seek profit (rewards) while incurring the least cost (payback).

4.4   Interpersonal communication and assertiveness

assertiveness

The third factor we have selected to explore in this unit is the role of **assertiveness** in the development of interpersonal relationships. The way in which we express ourselves to others, especially in the sensitive areas of feelings, needs and opinions, can have a positive or negative effect on the quality of our interpersonal relationships. Emotions such as anger, fear, happiness or sadness, as well as the feelings that arise when confronted with adversity and conflict, are all part of meaningful relationships. To build trust, engage in self-disclosure, resolve conflicts, express our needs, and influence others, we need to be able to communicate such feelings. Often, it is not the emotion itself that threatens (or enhances) the relationship, rather how you deal with the emotion, and the effect that it has on you and those who are important to you. Sometimes, problems are created in relationships with friends, family or work colleagues because we lack the communication skills needed to express our emotions, needs and opinions assertively. We may choose instead to bury them, or unleash them uncontrollably. The way we handle such feelings often impedes the relationship and creates additional conflicts instead of helping it (Gamble & Gamble 1987).

assertiveness

Verderber (1990:155) defines **assertiveness** as "verbalising your position on an issue for purposes of achieving a specific goal". The specific goal is to express yourself in such a way that you hurt neither yourself nor others. Assertiveness involves the ability to express feelings and opinions openly and honestly, to give good reasons for a belief or feeling, and to offer suggestions without attacking the other person verbally. Put another way, you have to be able to stand up for personal rights while respecting the rights of others. At the same time, the words you use and the manner in which you convey them should clearly indicate that you accept responsibility for what you say and how you say it.

4.4.1 Assertiveness styles

A study of the results of assertion training programmes leads Rakos (1986:408) to the conclusion that "assertion is a *skill*, not a 'trait' that someone 'has' or 'lacks'". As we pointed out in the Introduction to this book, skills can be learned, especially when we understand the theoretical principles on which they are grounded. While we may not be able to teach you the most appropriate language to use in each emotionally charged or adverse situation in your life, you will find that an understanding of the different ways or communication styles of **coping** with such situations will automatically make the choice of words much easier. The three possible communication styles in which you may express yourself are: passively (or nonassertively), aggressively, and assertively (Gamble & Gamble 1987; Dickson, Hargie & Morrow 1989; Verderber 1990).

passive style

▶ **The passive or nonassertive style:** People who behave *passively* suppress their feelings to avoid conflict or rejection, or are afraid to let others know how they are feeling, even when they are being treated unfairly. They are generally reluctant to state opinions, share feelings, or assume responsibility for their actions. They often submit to the demands of others even when it is not in their best interests. When people behave passively, they force themselves to keep their real feelings inside and frequently end up in relationships that they do not really want. You may have noticed that people who respond in a **nonassertive** style often hesitate, avoid eye contact, appease others, avoid contentious issues, accept blame needlessly, and generally lack confidence.

Experience shows that we hesitate to assert ourselves in our relationships for a number of different reasons which include a lack of interest in the relationship, fear at arousing the anger of our partner and subsequent reprisal, the feeling that we do not have language skills to express ourselves adequately, or because we sometimes experience feelings of personal inadequacy (a lack of self-worth) (Zimbardo & Radl 1979).

According to Furnham (1979), cultural differences also play a part in passive behaviour in that some cultures value assertiveness whereas others emphasise values of humility, tolerance and subservience. For example, in most societies, nonassertive behaviour is perceived to be an asset for women but a liability for men. Thus, some women behave passively because they accept the stereotype that society has taught them: they are expected to be accepting, warm, loving and deferential to men. However, this picture is changing in many parts of the world where the feminist movement has encouraged women to empower themselves and become far more assertive.

Both men and women sometimes lack assertiveness as a result of childhood experiences of authoritarian parents and teachers who discouraged the expression of personal opinions and feelings. For similar reasons, many people in the work situation, for instance, believe that they must always do what their superiors tell them, irrespective of the right or wrong of the situation. The problems of black men and women in South Africa have been exacerbated by the apartheid regime under which they were socialised and educated.

aggressive style

▶ **The aggressive style:** People who behave aggressively lash out at the source of their discomfort with little concern for the situation or the feelings of those *aggressive behaviour*

concerned. They insist on standing up for their own rights while ignoring or violating the rights of others. Their only concern is to dominate and 'win' in a relationship. Too many people confuse aggressiveness with assertiveness. Unlike assertiveness, **aggressive behaviour** is judgemental, dogmatic, faultfinding and coercive. The individual who responds in an aggressive style is often overbearing and self-opinionated, speaks loudly and abusively, interrupts others, and expresses opinions vehemently. They precipitate conflict, rather than resolve it. People can also be indirectly aggressive by subtly manipulating others. They very often display behaviour such as sulking, banging doors or drawers shut, or making the other person feel guilty.

According to assertiveness researchers, we tend to lash out at others simply because we have never been taught to handle our aggressive impulses, or because it acts as a form of self-defence when we feel vulnerable and powerless, or because we believe that the only way to get our ideas and feelings across to others is by being sufficiently forceful. It has also been noted that sometimes people who have repeatedly behaved in a passive manner in the past are no longer able to keep feelings of hurt and disappointment to themselves and abruptly vent them as aggressiveness (Lange & Jakubowski 1976).

assertive style

▶ **The assertive style:** The goal of **assertive behaviour** is neither to avoid conflict nor to dominate a relationship, but to communicate feelings and opinions honestly and clearly without hurting yourself or others. If passive and aggressive behaviour are partly due to inappropriate communication behaviours, we should be able to improve our interpersonal relationships by learning about assertive styles of behaviour.

People who behave assertively take responsibility for their actions and feelings without personal attacks on others or exaggerating for dramatic effect. They use a firm but conversational tone to express their feelings, to state what they believe to be true, to make suggestions about the behaviour or attitudes of others, and to give good reasons for their opinions and feelings. Their verbal and nonverbal messages are congruent. Thus, tone of voice, eye contact and posture match the words that are spoken. The individual who responds in an assertive style addresses contentious issues, is self-respecting, protects the rights of others, allows room for negotiation or compromise, and generally conveys confidence.

You have probably realised by now that when you assert yourself, you are protecting yourself from being victimised in a relationship. At the same time, you have to understand that **all people** have the same fundamental right. All of us have a right to protect ourselves, to express our needs in a relationship, and to influence the way others behave towards us. In essence, assertive behaviour implies that we have to find **mutually satisfactory solutions** to the problems and conflicts that arise in our relationships.

Being assertive may not always achieve the desired goal, but it is more likely to be successful than passive or aggressive behaviour. People who constantly display direct or indirect aggressive behaviour in interpersonal (or social) situations may initially get their own way, but they are generally disliked and their behaviour has a negative result on their relationships. On the other hand, people who constantly fail to assert themselves encourage others to manipulate them as they are perceived as weak and incompetent. Assertive people are generally respected and seen as competent, strong, fair and confident.

4.4.2   Developing assertive behaviour

Training yourself to improve assertive behaviour is not easy. It is certainly worth the effort. As Briggs (1986:24) maintains: "[a]ssertion training is about improving personal, and thereby professional, effectiveness. It is concerned with the building of self-confidence and esteem, and the ability to translate this into improving communications and relationships."

knowledge

Knowledge is a primary prerequisite for improving effective assertiveness in relationships. Understanding the nature of assertiveness, the different types of possible responses to adversity, and the reasons for not asserting ourselves will go a long way in helping us to understand our particular problems in this regard.

self-knowledge

Self-knowledge is also required. The discussion of perception in unit 3 is pertinent here. People may be unassertive because of mistaken perceptions of others, such as perceiving a tyrant as being a 'strong leader'. One way of understanding yourself with regard to assertive behaviour is to write down several situations in the past where you were nonassertive or aggressive. Try to determine the reasons for the behaviour and then substitute an assertive response for the nonassertive or aggressive behaviour in each case. Finally, try to transfer what you have learned to your everyday social (and work) situations.

assertiveness techniques

The exercise above can be facilitated by understanding that there are different techniques for asserting oneself in different situations. **Direct assertion** involves a short, straightforward statement in support of one's opinions, suggestions or rights. In **indirect assertion** the person does not actually confront the issue, but indirectly states her point of view. In **complex-direct assertion**, the person uses an embellishment to soften the situation. The main types of embellishment are: showing *empathy* towards the other person; the use of *praise*; giving an *apology* for any negative consequences; or suggesting a *compromise*.

To illustrate the different techniques, we quote the examples provided by Dickson, Hargie and Morrow (1989:119–120). The scenario the authors use is that of refusing an invitation to deliver a paper at a conference, yet protecting the relationship with the other person.

1 **Direct:** 'No, I can't undertake such a commitment at this time';

2 **Indirect:** 'Phew ... I've got so much on my plate at the moment; I have a deadline to meet on two books and I know I have another commitment around that time ...';

3 **Complex-direct:**

    (a) 'I couldn't undertake this commitment, since I am behind with the deadline on a forthcoming book, and I already have another speaking engagement in June.' *(explanation)*;

    (b) 'I know you have a lot on your plate organising the conference but ...' *(empathy)*;

    (c) 'It's really nice of you to ask me and if I could do it for you I would ...' *(praise)*;

    (d) 'I'm sorry to give you more problems in organising speakers, but ...' *(apology)*;

    (e) 'I can't undertake this but I have a colleague whom I think could ...' *(compromise)*.

nonverbal behaviour

You should also consider your **nonverbal behaviour** in assertive situations. The role of nonverbal communication (for example, eye contact, tone of voice, facial expressions, gestures and posture) in conveying attitudes and influencing relationships is discussed in unit 2. It is very difficult, for instance, to assert yourself in a contentious situation if you constantly avoid eye contact with the person with whom you are interacting.

To conclude this section on developing assertiveness, we provide what Gamble and Gamble (1987:192) conceive as *Every Person's Bill of Rights*. The authors point out that when we sacrifice our rights, we teach others to take advantage of us. When we demand rights that are not ours, we take advantage of others. Their bill of rights offers guidelines on how to stand up for your emotional rights without being insensitive to the rights and feelings of others.

1 The right to be treated with respect

2 The right to make your own choices and decisions

3 The right to make mistakes and/or change your mind

4 The right to have needs and to have these needs considered as important as the needs of others

5 The right to express your feelings and opinions

6 The right to judge your own behaviour

7   The right to set your own priorities

8   The right to say no without feeling guilty

9   The right not to make choices for others

10 The right not to assert yourself

Case 4.1

This case is adapted from Verderber (1993).

Kim, Brenda and Shirley are first-year students who live in the same residence at the university they are attending. The three girls are very excited as they prepare for the annual dance that evening. When the three young men who are to be their partners at the dance arrive to call for them, Chris reaches into his pocket for a flask of whisky, takes a large sip, and passes the bottle to Brenda. They all know that alcohol is not allowed in the residence rooms and, in any case, Brenda is concerned about anyone in the group drinking before driving. She doesn't know what to do because she does not want to precipitate an unpleasant incident before the start of what should be an exciting evening. She mutters "Uh, er, well," as she pretends to take a sip and passes the bottle on.

Kim grabs the bottle and says, "Chris, you bloody idiot — that's damn stupid, bringing whisky into our residence. Can't anybody here have a good time without drinking? You're all impossible. Now get out of here before somebody notices, and take the bottle with you."

Seeing the angry look on Chris's face, Shirley quickly says, "Chris, perhaps you didn't know that drinking is not allowed in this residence. Besides, I'd feel a lot better if we all stayed sober in order to drive to the dance. So I'd appreciate it if you'd lock the whisky in the boot of the car. We can have a great time without getting into trouble or risking an accident."

After you have studied the case, answer the following questions.

1   Which of the three responses can be described as *(a)* assertive, *(b)* passive, *(c)* aggressive?

2   Is the passive response in the interests of the group? What is the possible outcome?

3 Is the aggressive response in the interests of the group? What is the possible outcome?

4 Is the assertive response in the interests of the group? What is the possible outcome?

5 Comment briefly on the following: the feelings you think are being expressed in the three responses; the choice of language; and the nonverbal behaviour that probably accompanied each response (including paralanguage).

Summary

Interpersonal communication is communication between two (or more) people in a face-to-face encounter. In this unit we have examined communication between two people by focusing on the relationships that we develop and maintain in our everyday lives. The link between interpersonal communication and our mode of existence was discussed by examining Martin Buber's *I-you* and *I-it* relationships. We then looked at three factors that influence the development and nature of our relationships: listening, interpersonal needs and communication style. We emphasised the importance of efficient listening in interpersonal relationships and then referred to the theories of Schutz and Homans to explain the role of needs in interpersonal relationships. Schutz discusses inclusion, affection and control as interpersonal needs, while Homans focuses on social exchange. We discussed passive, aggressive and assertive communication styles. Throughout the unit, we provided some guidelines to help improve our interpersonal relationships. The unit ended with a case study based on three different communication styles.

Test-yourself

1 Define the following terms with specific reference to interpersonal communication:

(a) *I-you* relationship

(b) *I-it* relationship

(c)   listening

(d)   interpersonal needs

(e)   passive communication

(f)   assertive communication

(g)   aggressive communication

2   Explain the function of feedback in the listening process.

3   Think of a situation in which you let a personal prejudice interfere with your listening. How did this prejudice interfere with your communication encounter? Explain your answer briefly.

4   Think about some of your current and past relationships and apply the theories we have been discussing to help you gain more insight into your own and your partners' needs in interpersonal relationships. In terms of Schutz's theory, how balanced are your needs for inclusion, affection and control? How have these needs motivated you to communicate with another person? Then think about whether some of the relationships you have maintained provide you with greater need fulfilment than cost. In those relationships you have terminated, were the costs greater than the profits? Finally, turn your attention to the role that your communication style may have played in the maintenance or termination of some of your relationships.

5   Write passive, aggressive and assertive responses to each of the scenarios described below.

(a)   A friend invites you to accompany her to a movie you do not want to see.

(b)   Your supervisor wants you to take your annual leave at a time that does not suit you because you have already made plans to go on holiday with friends.

(c) You have loaned a book to a friend who seems to have forgotten to give it back. You do not need the book urgently, but are worried about never receiving it if you do not raise the issue.

(d) Your mother/father constantly makes comments that you find hurtful because he/she does not like the way you dress.

What do you think would be the possible outcomes of each response?

Suggested reading

Alberti, RE & Emmons, ML. 1986. *Your perfect right: a guide to assertive living.* 5th edition. Calif: Impact

Brownell, J. 1986. *Building active listening skills.* Englewood Cliffs, NJ: Prentice-Hall.

Buber, M. 1970. *I and Thou.* Edinburgh: Clark.

Homans, GC. 1950. *The human group.* New York: Harcourt, Brace & World.

Homans, GC. 1961. *Social behaviour: its elementary forms.* New York: Harcourt, Brace & World.

Knapp, ML. 1984. *Interpersonal communication and human relationships.* Newton, Maine: Allyn & Bacon.

Lange, AJ & Jakubowski, P. 1976. *Responsible assertive behaviour.* Champaign, Ill: Research.

Luft, J. 1969. *Of human interaction.* Palo Alto, Calif: National Press.

Lustig, MW & Koester, J. 1993. *Intercultural competence: interpersonal communication across cultures.* New York: HarperCollins

Roloff, ME & Miller, GR. 1987. *Interpersonal processes: new directions in communication research.* Beverly Hills, Calif: Sage.

Schutz, WC. 1969. *The interpersonal underworld.* Reading, Mass: Addison-Wesley.

Van der Merwe, N. 1991. *Listening: a skill for everyone.* Cape Town: Arrow.

Wolff, FI, Marsnik, NC, Tacey, WS & Nichols, RG. 1983. *Perceptive listening.* New York: Holt, Rinehart & Winston.

Zimbardo, PG & Radl, SL. 1979. *The shyness workbook.* New York: The A&W Visual Library.

Small-group communication

Overview

All of us spend some of our time in groups. Think for a moment about your daily activities and the different groups to which you belong. As a child, a large part of your socialisation process occurred in your family and school groups. As an adult, you probably belong to a social or sports club, religious group, study group, support group, or work group at your place of employment. These examples tell us that some groups are *socially oriented*; they stem from the human need for social contact. Other groups are *task oriented*; the group works towards achieving a specific aim such as solving a problem or arriving at a decision. Of course, the categories often overlap: a social group such as a tennis club may have to solve the problem of raising funds to send a team on tour, for example, while many institutional task groups arrange social events for their members. Nevertheless, all groups, regardless of their function, have similar patterns of communication that affect how the members act, speak and communicate with each other.

In this unit, we focus primarily on *task groups*, sometimes referred to as *committees*. After defining a small group, we point out the advantages and disadvantages of small groups. We then consider the characteristics of effective groups and the types of roles that group members play. We examine the important role played by the leader of a group and point out some guidelines for becoming an efficient leader. We then discuss different types of communication networks that operate in small groups and the conse-quences of each. This is followed by an examination of the ways groups discuss the problems they have to address and the decisions that are made. The final section of the unit points out the main differences between interpersonal and small-group communication, and the unit ends with a case study which is based on a problem-solving sequence that can be used by a small group.

Learning outcomes

At the end of this unit you should be able to do the following.

1   Define a *small group.*

2   Enumerate the advantages and disadvantages of small groups.

3   Provide examples of how *climate* affects the operation of a group.

4   Explain how *groupthink* encourages conformity.

5   Define *group role.*

6   Define and give two examples of *task, maintenance* and *self-centred* roles.

7   Describe and explain the steps in a group discussion. Use your own example of a problem-solving situation.

8   Distinguish between questions of fact, value and policy, and give an example of each.

9   Define and briefly describe the technique *brainstorming.*

10 Define leadership and list five characteristics that typify a good leader.

11 Distinguish among three leadership styles and give an example of each.

12 Describe how leadership theories contribute to our knowledge and understanding of leadership.

13 Apply the knowledge you have gained in this unit in the small groups to which you belong.

14 Answer the questions based on the case at the end of this unit.

Introduction

We live in a society where being part of a group, or several groups, is not a matter of choice — it is inescapable. We choose to belong to some groups (for example a sports club) and have others assigned to us by birth (for example family, age, gender). Our choice of groups and the way we behave in them depends on several factors. You may fulfil personal needs, for example, by joining a youth group, but the way you participate in the group is shaped, to a large extent, not only by the conventions of the group, but by your culture. As a white Western female, your involvement in a youth group is relatively unrestricted and it is accepted that you will interact with the males in the group. But, for an Asian female, such behaviour is not always acceptable and is often forbidden (Burton & Dimbleby 1995).

Groups are essential in helping society to function efficiently. For example, the government achieves many of its goals by appointing groups or committees to investigate and propose legislation. On a personal level, there are also many benefits to be gained from participation in groups. Belonging to a support group such as Alcoholics Anonymous or Weigh Less, for instance, in which members of the group share experiences and offer one another support, has helped many people to overcome undesirable drinking and eating habits. Professional success is often measured by how effectively a person contributes to task groups, especially in a leadership capacity.

The main form of communication in a small group is discussion. Group members in an organisation, for instance, meet to exchange information about a situation, make a decision about an issue, or solve a problem. Discussion is important because it is a way for everyone to participate and voice an opinion. Barker and Gaut (1996:156) maintain that "The existence of small groups is a basic part of the democratic process."

However, people are often reluctant to attend group discussions or to participate in them. One of the main complaints is that meetings are a waste of time because they seldom accomplish as much as they should. Often, the ineffectiveness of the group is blamed on the leader but, as Verderber (1990) points out, the responsibility for the 'waste of time' in fact lies with the individual members. Studying group processes — that is, how group members communicate and interact with each other — can help you to make better use of the time you spend in groups and can also help you to participate more effectively in the different groups to which you belong.

5.1 Defining a group

Arriving at a scientific definition of a group is not easy. A group is not simply a random collection of individuals who happen to occupy a particular space at the same time. Thus, six people waiting at a bus stop or riding together in an elevator is not considered a group. Neither is fifty or a hundred people watching a film together in a cinema. A **group** is a collection of individuals who see themselves as **belonging** to the group, who **interact** verbally and nonverbally, who occupy certain **roles** with respect to one another, and who cooperate to accomplish a definite **goal**. A **small group** is composed of three to twelve people interacting face to face in such a way that each person influences and is influenced by every other person in the group (Barker & Gaut 1996; Gamble & Gamble 1987).

group/ small group

Let's consider the six people waiting for a bus. Certainly, they have a common goal; they are all waiting for a bus. But there is no need to interact with one another to accomplish this goal. Should an accident occur in the street where they are waiting, however, and they begin discussing how to obtain help for the accident victims, they would become a group rather than a random collection of people. During their interaction, they would decide such matters as who should telephone for an ambulance, who should fetch blankets to cover the victims, and who should try to keep them quiet until help arrives. Their unified effort would make them a small group for the duration of their interaction.

The specific goals for which a small group strives may vary: for instance, a family meets to plan the household budget; a student committee meets to plan a strategy for improving hostel conditions; a study group meets to help its members to understand course work; a board of directors meets to plan corporate policy for the coming year; union members meet to discuss contract demands. Although their goals vary, for each of these groups to succeed its members must work together effectively. Their understanding of group dynamics (the scientific study of small groups), as well as the way the members communicate with each other will, to a large extent, determine the effectiveness of the group. Gamble and Gamble (1987) maintain that knowing how to communicate with others in a group setting is vital if you are to attain personal success, and critical if you are to attain professional success. While you study this section, you should bear in mind that everything you have learned about communication so far applies to small groups. Because small-group communication is more complex than two-person communication, additional knowledge and skills are required and are discussed in the remainder of this section.

We begin by looking at some of the advantages and disadvantages of small groups, and then discuss features that characterise small groups, as well as the roles that group members fulfil.

5.2 Advantages and disadvantages of small groups

Groups that meet to solve problems and reach decisions have both advantages and disadvantages. Research shows that the ***advantages*** of small groups include the following.

advantages

▶ People who work in groups usually accomplish more than people who work alone because the individual members of the group can pool resources and information to achieve goals and reach decisions. Let's say that a university committee is considering the feasibility of establishing tutorial groups for students who study at a distance. Different members of the group can gather information such as: how many students would be likely to attend? In which areas? Are there tutors in the selected subjects? Is there adequate accommodation for the tutorial groups? How much would the enterprise cost? Would additional staff be required? It is often extremely difficult for one person to obtain all the information in a short time. The more information that is made available to the group, the more likely they are to arrive at a good decision or effective solution.

▶ Working in a group rather than alone usually results in an increase in individual motivation to find a solution to a problem, as well as greater commitment to the task on hand. There seems to be a desire not to let the group down.

▶ Superior decisions and solutions are often reached because groups are generally better equipped than individuals to foresee difficulties, detect weaknesses, visualise consequences and explore possibilities. Often the group can pinpoint errors in an individual member's thinking and discuss and rectify them before additional problems are created.

▶ The decisions or solutions arrived at by a group tend to be better received by others than those made by an individual. The fact that a number of people came to one conclusion appears to command respect from those to whom the group reports.

▶ Many people find that working in a group is more pleasant and fulfilling than working alone. The knowledge that others respect their opinions and are willing to confirm their ideas provides a feeling of personal satisfaction.

disadvantages

Despite the strong points of using groups to solve problems and make decisions, certain drawbacks have also been identified. The **disadvantages** of groups include the following.

▶ There is a temptation for some people to sit back and allow others to do all the work. Such people seem to have a knack for avoiding duties and responsibilities, yet still take credit for the group's achievements.

▶ On the other hand, there is a temptation for forceful people to take over and dominate the group. Such people often refuse to make compromises or allow others to be heard. The problem is exacerbated when lower-status members are reluctant to criticise the ideas of someone who is of higher status.

▶ The personal goals of group members sometimes conflict with group goals to the extent that they interfere with group objectives. An individual member who is seeking promotion, for example, might use the group to further his own ends. In the example of the university committee above, for instance, a member might recruit tutors in a particular area as quickly as possible to show how competent he is, without taking the main goal of the group into account — in this case, to determine the feasibility of establishing tutorial groups in the first place.

▶ It generally takes longer for a group to reach a decision than an individual working alone. In business and industry, where time is money, and where it is often essential to reach a decision quickly, the group process can be a disadvantage (Gamble & Gamble 1987).

The consensus of opinion is that when the problem to be solved is simple, it is more efficient for one person to work alone, but in a complex or difficult situation, there are advantages to having people pool their resources, knowledge and insight.

5.3 Group characteristics

A question that is often asked in connection with the study of small groups is: what makes an effective group? Research shows that effective small groups generally have an optimum number of members, have a good working environment, show cohesiveness, have a commitment to the task, respect norms, and meet key role requirements (Gamble & Gamble 1987; Hamilton & Parker 1990; Verderber 1990; Tubbs & Moss 1991).

5.3.1 Optimum number of members

Our definition of a small group in section 5.1 makes it clear that the interactions of individual members are important for the group to function efficiently. The members must be able to talk to each other and discuss ideas that are put forward. That is why a small group is limited to about twelve people. If the group becomes too large, the members cannot fully participate in the discussion. In fact, research indicates that, although optimum size depends on the nature of the task, five to seven people is the most productive size. Such a group is large enough to supply information and to share the work-load, but small enough to give each member the opportunity for maximum participation. An odd number is preferable in a group of any size because, if the group finds it necessary to vote on an issue on which it cannot achieve consensus, the odd number will prevent tie votes.

5.3.2 Good working environment

A good working environment is one that promotes interaction among its members. Apart from a pleasant physical environment, such as a room with adequate heating in winter, an important consideration is seating. Seating that is too formal or too informal inhibits free discussion. The leader who sits at the head of a long table, for example, may be perceived as the 'boss' in charge of proceedings and often inhibits participation from the group. On the other hand, when the seating is too informal, subgroups of two or three people may form within the group and also not participate fully. The ideal arrangement is to have a circular table or an arrangement of tables that makes a square, so that everyone can see everyone else. In terms of seating position, everyone has equal status which establishes a climate in which all members have equal opportunity to participate.

group climate

The *climate* referred to here concerns the atmosphere created in the group and is largely dependent on the communication styles of the members. Your own experience probably tells you that some groups have 'too hot' a climate in that members are intolerant of each other and quickly lose their tempers, while others have 'too cold' a climate in that members are aloof, sarcastic, and generally unconcerned about hurting one another's feelings or ensuring that everyone gets the opportunity to voice an opinion. It has been found that members tend to act in a way that reinforces the prevailing group climate. Redding (1972) suggests that an effective group climate has the following ingredients: (1) supportiveness; (2) participative decision-making; (3) trust among group members; (4) openness and candour; and (5) high performance goals.

Group climate also affects the cohesiveness and commitment of the members to the task in hand and to group norms.

5.3.3 Cohesiveness and commitment to the task

commitment

Commitment describes the willingness of individual members to work together to complete the group's task. Without sufficient commitment, there is little chance of success. People have different degrees of commitment to group work. When the group believes that what it is doing is important, members are more inclined to give fully of their time and energy. Groups that succeed in meeting their goals have members who are committed to the group in terms of attending meetings, doing what is expected of them, and striving to meet the group's goals.

cohesiveness

homogeneous
consisting of like
parts/people

heterogeneous
consisting of
unlike parts/
people

When members are committed, the group is likely to be cohesive. ***Cohesiveness*** means pulling together or uniting to accomplish a task. Effective groups are usually cohesive in that individual members actively work together as a group, and help one another as group members. A homogeneous group is generally more cohesive than a heterogeneous group. A ***homogeneous*** group is one in which the members have a great deal in common and pursue similar needs and purposes. A group of five women of similar age and background who are all against abortion would be a homogeneous group. A ***heterogeneous*** group is one in which different ages, backgrounds and interests are represented. Cohesiveness is also directly related to the belief of individual members that are they liked, that they are accepted in the group, and that their opinions are respected. Group cohesiveness usually makes it easier for the group to find ways to reach consensus when problems have to be solved and decisions made.

There is, however, the danger of too much cohesion within a group, especially if the group has a strong, dominant and respected leader. Too much cohesion can lead group members to be so concerned with maintaining good relationships within the group that they neglect the purpose for which they came together. The result is that the group is not open to new ideas and may not allow new members to **groupthink** join. Such groups suffer from **groupthink** — a condition where minimising conflict and preserving harmony are more important goals than the critical examination of ideas. When groupthink predominates, the group as a whole tends to discount negative information and may even ignore ethical considerations to preserve cohesiveness. Groupthink also affects individuals within the group. Since non-conformity might damage cohesion, members who privately disagree with the views expressed by the majority may be unwilling to risk conflict by publicly admitting that they disagree. The outcome of groupthink can be that group decisions turn out to be unfair, discriminatory or insensitive (Janis 1972; Ellis & McClintock 1994).

Groupthink has influenced decisions that range from political actions to a cult group's choice of clothing. During the Second World War, for instance, Roosevelt's close-knit presidential team ignored disturbing information that was passed on to them because, in their view, it was not possible for Pearl Harbour — the American naval base in Hawaii — to be bombed by the Japanese. Burton and Dimbleby (1995) also link groupthink with ideologies. Religious and political groups over the centuries have wanted to believe that their value system is right and all others are wrong. Calvinists, for instance, believed that only their followers would go to heaven. The problem is that when people 'know' that they belong to the only 'right' ideological group, their belief may be used to justify all sorts of behaviour to others.

5.3.4 Group norms

norms

Norms are the explicit and implicit rules for behaviour that are established to enable the group to operate effectively and to develop cohesiveness. In other words, groups develop standards of behaviour to which they expect members to conform. Some norms are formal or written, such as the clearly stated codes of conduct laid down for the medical profession. Others norms are informal or unwritten, and are established early on in the group's meetings. Two important areas of norm development are group interaction and group procedure. To describe **group interaction**, think about the following examples: you may, for instance, belong to one group in which it is acceptable to interrupt the speaker to ask questions, or openly express support or disagreement with a member; on the other hand, you may belong to another group in which members are expected to be quiet until discussion is invited. Similarly, in one group the **procedure** may be that business is not discussed unless everyone is present; in another, it may be accepted that some people come late or leave early. Norms vary from group to group and most are learned through experience with a specific group. Once established and reinforced, norms that are detrimental to the group (such as being unpunctual, using expletives, and interrupting the speaker) are difficult to change. Being aware of the potential of such behaviour to detract from the effectiveness of a group encourages members to cooperate in preventing detrimental norms to develop in the first place.

group interaction

group procedure

5.3.5 Filling role requirements

role

The concept *role* is borrowed from the stage, where it refers to the character played by an actor in a play. In the social sciences, a **role** is defined as a pattern of behaviour that is appropriate for a person's position in a group. In other words, members of a group fulfil certain prescribed roles and are accorded status according to the role they play. In every group, for instance, there is a leader who is responsible for the functioning of the group. The leader becomes the central figure in the group 'drama', with the other members acting as peripheral characters around him. In effective groups, the members understand and fill the various roles that enable the group to function. The specific role of group leadership is discussed in section 5.4. In this section, we point out the general functions of people who fulfil task roles, maintenance roles and self-centred roles, a classification first suggested by Benne and Sheats (1948). Note that task and maintenance roles have a positive function in the group, whereas self-centred roles are dysfunctional or negative.

task roles

Task roles reflect the work a group must do to accomplish its goals. People who fulfil task roles initiate ideas, seek and provide information, define problems, clarify and summarise suggestions and proposals, and record the group's key decisions. Task roles are not limited to any one individual but are usually interchanged among the members.

maintenance roles

Maintenance roles reflect the group behaviours that keep the group working together smoothly. People who perform maintenance roles fulfil the emotional needs of the group. They support and encourage others by offering praise or agreement, relieve tension by helping group members to reconcile differences, control conflict, and act as gatekeeper by keeping lines of communication open and seeing that everyone has a chance to participate.

self-centred roles

Problems arise in small-group communication when members deliberately play ***self-centred roles*** — roles that accomplish egocentric or self-serving functions. They achieve this by being aggressive, seeking attention, promoting personal interests, or not contributing at all. People who fulfil such roles dominate the discussion, verbally attack others, clown around, block suggestions, and engage in point-picking — criticising everything the group attempts.

People who play task and maintenance roles are aware of the importance of participation in small groups — the need to interact with other members of the group. Responsible group members tend to plan what they are going to say in advance so that they can present their suggestions clearly and logically; they listen attentively, taking note of both the verbal and nonverbal elements of the message; and they try to provide constructive feedback rather than dismiss the ideas of other group members.

In the following section, we concentrate on the role of the group leader.

5.4 Leadership in groups

Groups sometimes operate effectively without a designated leader. Most groups, especially those engaged in problem-solving, need effective leadership to achieve their goals. *Leadership* is defined as any behaviour that facilitates group task accomplishment, and a *leader* is any person with the ability to influence others. *Influence* means bringing about changes in the attitudes and actions of others. It differs from the exercise of raw power in that a good leader does not force people to submit to a particular point of view. A skilful leader **guides** the group through a discussion, pointing out the advantages and limitations of all the ideas suggested by the members so that the best outcome can be reached.

leadership/ leader

Leaders are either designated by the group, or they achieve leadership because they exhibit leadership behaviours. Effective leaders are able to help a group attain both task and maintenance functions. For example, they contribute to establishing a group climate that encourages and stimulates interaction; they take responsibility for ensuring that group communication proceeds smoothly; they ask relevant questions, offer summaries as the discussion proceeds, and encourage the group to continually evaluate and improve its performance (Gamble & Gamble 1987; Hamilton & Parker 1990; Verderber 1990).

5.4.1 Leadership theories

Of the many theories that have been developed about leadership, we have selected two for discussion: leadership traits and leadership styles (Barker 1984; Verderber 1990).

Leadership traits

Early researchers assumed that leaders are born, not made, and looked for personality traits that distinguish leaders from nonleaders. One such study revealed that effective leaders display consistent traits which relate to ability, sociability, motivation and communication skills. With regard to **ability**, leaders generally exceed average group members in intelligence, scholarship, insight and verbal facility. Sociability traits include dependability, activeness, cooperation and popularity. In the area of motivation leaders generally exceed nonleaders in initiative, persistence and enthusiasm. Leaders also reveal a high level of competency in a variety of communication skills. A later study revealed five behaviours that **prevent** people from becoming leaders: being uninformed about the problem under discussion; being too rigid in opinions about the problem; not participating; being too authoritarian or 'bossy'; and being verbally offensive — talking too much or talking in a pompous way.

Such traits and behaviours are generalisations, and it does not follow that people who exhibit leadership traits will become group leaders. Research indicates that no one set of characteristics is common to all leaders, and that leaders and followers alike share many of the same characteristics. The particular situation appears to determine in part which individual comes forward to exert leadership. The value of trait research is that it provides **indicators of potential leadership**. Thus, while it is not valid to say that leaders **must** have particular traits, it is valid to conclude that **certain traits** are more likely to be found in leaders than nonleaders. Regarding traits as indicators of good leadership is also useful in that it refutes the notion that some people are destined to become leaders. The prevailing view is that most people can be **trained** to be good leaders.

Leadership styles

Very often the quality of work produced by groups depends on the set of behaviours or style of leadership of the group leader. The assumptions we make about how people work together will influence the type of leadership style we adopt. Some leaders assume that the average group member is inherently lazy, prefers to avoid responsibility, and must be closely supervised. Others assume that the average group member enjoys work, is self-directed, and will willingly assume responsibility (McGregor 1960). These assumptions have resulted in the identification of three different leadership styles: authoritarian, democratic and laissez-faire styles.

authoritarian leaders

Authoritarian leaders are strongly task-oriented and have firm opinions on how to achieve the group's goals. They exercise direct control over the group by determining policy and procedure, assigning tasks and roles to members, and deciding who may talk and who may not. An authoritarian leader often makes decisions without consulting the group. Although such an approach may be effective during crisis situations as it produces fast decisions, the usual outcome of this style is that it causes conflict within the group and group satisfaction is low.

democratic leaders

Democratic leaders are people-oriented. They guide rather than direct a group by involving all members in discussion and debate and letting everyone's points of view be heard. While such a leader may suggest alternatives, it is left to the group to decide on specific policy, procedure, and the tasks and roles of members. Democratic leadership has been proven to produce high quality results as it provides opportunities for originality and creativity, and stimulates group cohesiveness, motivation to work and achieve goals, and the desire to communicate.

The results of studies reported by White and Lippert (1960) suggest the following advantages and disadvantages of each style.

▶ The least amount of work is done when no leadership exists.

▶ More work is done under a task leader than under a person-oriented leader.

▶ Task leadership may create discontent and/or result in less individuality.

▶ Motivation and originality are greater under a person-centred leader.

▶ More friendliness is shown in person-oriented groups.

*laissez-faire
leaders*

The third type is ***laissez-faire leadership***. Such leaders generally adopt a 'let them do their own thing' attitude and try not to direct the group at all. They supply information, advice and material when asked, but do not actively participate in group decisions. The group has complete freedom in determining policy, procedure, tasks and roles. While members of a laissez-faire group feel free to progress and develop on their own, they may often be distracted from the task at hand and suffer loss of direction. The result is that the quality of work they produce suffers. On the other hand, this kind of leadership is appropriate in situations where too much direction would stifle group creativity. Support groups, such as groups for the terminally ill, seem to work well under this type of leadership because the members come together for the purpose of helping each other, and prefer not be tied to a particular procedure or structure.

Although the democratic style of leadership is preferred by most people who participate in groups, all three leadership styles can be effective under the appropriate conditions. When an urgent decision is required, for example, the authoritarian style may serve the group's best interests. In situations where a minimum of interference may produce the best results, the laissez-faire style is recommended. When commitment to the group decision is of the greatest importance, the democratic style should be practised. In other words, there are no rigid rules. In this respect, give some consideration to the following thoughts on leadership provided by EM Estes, President of General Motors Corporation in the United States:

> Leadership is the courage to admit mistakes, the vision to welcome change, the enthusiasm to motivate others, and the confidence to stay out of step when everyone else is marching to the wrong tune.

5.4.2 Developing leadership skills

Whether you are elected as the leader of a group, or emerge as the leader, it is not possible to provide effective leadership unless you ensure that the group functions well and makes progress towards reaching its goals. Some points that group leaders should attend to in this respect include the following:

▶ having sufficient knowledge about the particular task;

▶ setting an example by working harder than anyone else in the group;

▶ showing sincerity by being personally committed to group goals and needs;

▶ being decisive at key moments in the discussion;

▶ interacting freely with all members of the group, but at the same time not dominating the discussion;

▶ developing skills in maintenance functions as well as task functions so that the group remains cohesive and functional.

Some guidelines for efficient leadership

Being a good leader also means being aware of and attending to the responsibilities of ensuring that a meeting proceeds as efficiently as possible. You should think about the following suggestions to facilitate efficient group leadership (Hybels & Weaver 1989; Hamilton & Parker 1990).

▶ Inform everyone involved when and where all meetings are to take place and distribute an agenda — a list of all the items that will be discussed during the meeting.

▶ Select a place for the meeting that will be conducive to discussion. For example, make sure that there are no distractions and that the seating arrangements invite participation by all members.

▶ Check the facilities shortly before the meeting to see that everything needed is in place. You may, for example, require an overhead projector, a tape recorder, or a chalkboard.

▶ Start on time and stick to the agenda to avoid wasting time.

▶ Preview the agenda briefly at the start of the meeting to make sure that everyone knows exactly what is to be discussed.

▶ Encourage discussion but ensure that no one person is allowed to monopolise the discussion.

▶ Ask pertinent questions. For example, if the group discussion goes off track, you should intervene with a question such as: is this directly related to the problem we are discussing? If information is to be evaluated, you should ask questions such as: how recent is the information? Who is the source? Might the source be biased?

▶ Summarise the main points as the discussion progresses and provide an overall summary at the end.

▶ Thank the participants (and audience, if any).

▶ Make sure that everyone who needs the results of the meeting is properly informed. If people are affected by the results of the meeting, inform them as quickly as possible.

5.5 Communication networks in small groups

Communication is the essential ingredient for the continued existence of a group. The group's ability to accomplish a task is related to the interactions of its members. Do they feel free to express themselves openly to each other and do they have the opportunity to receive feedback about their ideas? The structure of the group, or the relationship of members to each other in the group, plays a major role in the effectiveness of communication in the group. A way of looking at group structure is in terms of communication networks. **Communication networks** are recurring patterns of interaction or, stated simply, who talks to whom in a group? By examining networks, we examine where there are communication channels and which members transmit and receive messages to and from one another (Fisher 1981; Gamble & Gamble 1987; Trenholm 1991; Tubbs & Moss 1991).

communication networks

Figure 5.1: Communication networks

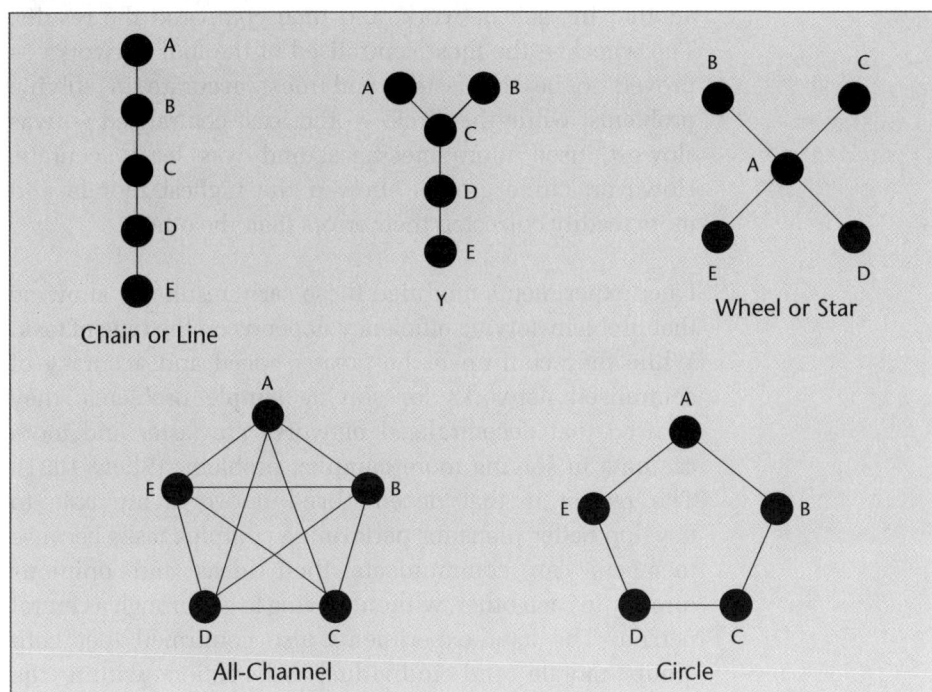

Chain or Line

Y

Wheel or Star

All-Channel

Circle

Figure 5.1 illustrates a number of networks that might exist in a five-member group. The wheel, chain and Y are **centralised networks**. In the wheel, A — who occupies the central position — is able to communicate with the other four, but they can communicate only with him or her. In the Y network, A, B and E can communicate with only one other person, and in the chain, the same applies to A and E. In centralised networks, the person with the most channels of communication tends to become the group leader. Unlike these networks, the circle and all-channel patterns are **decentralised** and sometimes leaderless. In the circle, each member is able to communicate with two others and, in the all-channel network, each member is able to communicate with all the others.

centralised networks

decentralised networks

Two early sociologists, Bavelas (1950) and Leavitt (1951) conducted research on small groups to measure the problem-solving abilities of different networks. They studied four communication patterns: the chain, wheel, Y, and circle. Leavitt manipulated the freedom with which information could be transmitted from one subject to another in each network, and then compared the results. The wheel — the most centralised of the four networks — proved to be the fastest and most accurate in solving problems, while the circle — the least centralised — was slowest, used more messages, and was least accurate. However, circle groups showed the highest morale and more readily corrected their errors than the others.

Later experiments modified these early results by showing that problem-solving efficiency depends on the **type of task**. While they confirmed the greater speed and accuracy of centralised networks for solving **simple** problems, they showed that decentralised networks are faster and more accurate in solving more **complex** problems (Shaw 1981). The reason is that decentralised networks are able to develop better plans for performing complex tasks because members can communicate their ideas and opinions directly to each other, without having to go through a central person. The later experiments also confirmed that both group morale and individual satisfaction within the operation of the group are higher when people are not cut off from each other. The general consensus among researchers is that the all-channel network seems to be the most desirable. While it initially tends to be more inefficient, the opportunities for free discussion and feedback ultimately result in greater accuracy and satisfaction.

It is important to be aware that experimental studies of communication networks are highly artificial and thus cannot be transferred directly to real-life groups. In the natural environment, factors such as noise, the location of information, and members' skills and previous experience would also play a role in solving problems. Nevertheless, network research helps us more readily to understand why some group members feel frustrated while others feel content, why some groups have a higher morale than others, and why some groups reach their goals more readily than others.

A good reason for creating open channels in small groups is that, as we mentioned in the introduction to this unit, communication about the real problems and decisions with which groups are faced is done through discussion among the members. Discussion provides an opportunity for several ideas to be proposed and either to be accepted, rejected or modified in response to group feedback. An understanding of communication networks can assist the leader of a group in eliciting contributions from all members and encourage open communication between them.

In the following two sections, we examine the way in which groups discuss problems and the qualities of an efficient group leader.

5.6 Discussion in groups

Group members meet formally or informally to exchange information and ideas in order to solve problems and make decisions. For instance, a school committee discusses how to raise money for new computers; a tenants' committee discusses ways of improving the apartment complex; a security group discusses safety arrangements for political leaders; a jury meets to arrive at a legal decision; most organisations in society have several groups that meet regularly to solve administrative problems that arise in the organisation.

Problem-solving and decision-making are joint activities. In order to make a decision about an issue, the problem has to be investigated. Problem-solving is the process by which people generate and evaluate the solutions to an identified problem so that the best one can be chosen and implemented (Brilhart 1989). According to Berko, Wolvin and Curtis (1986), a **good decision** is one that the decision-makers feel comfortable with, the solution that the group perceives to be the best possible one for the existing problem. In other words, the group reaches *consensus*. Consensus means that group members actively participate in a discussion until they are committed to a decision. It does not mean that all agree with the decision, but that all understand the decision, accept it, and will carry out their part in implementing it. While there are different approaches to problem-solving, researchers suggest that groups reach consensus more efficiently if they understand and follow a systematic procedure designed to lead them through the problem-solving process to a specific choice. The structure or sequence in figure 5.2 has been shown to work well in many problem-solving situations (Fisher 1981; Hybels & Weaver 1989; Tubbs & Moss 1991). There are five steps in the problem-solving process described below: (1) identifying and defining the problem; (2) analysing and researching the problem; (3) deciding what the solution should accomplish; (4) finding and evaluating solutions; (5) implementing the solution.

Figure 5.2: The problem-solving sequence

1. Identify and define the problem.	2. Analyse and research the problem.	3. Decide what the solution should accomplish.	4. Find and evaluate solutions.	5. Implement the solution.

5.6.1 Identifying and defining the problem

The first step is to recognise that a problem indeed exists and for the group as a whole to agree that it is a problem. Obvious problems such as 'We're out of money' are easy to identify and agree on. Sometimes, a symptom is mistaken for a problem. For instance, falling sales in a company may be due to a poorly designed product, and not to inadequate efforts on the part of the sales team. Members must understand the specific goal of the group to avoid the waste of time mentioned earlier. An efficient way of identifying a problem is to phrase it as a question. Basically there are three kinds of question: questions of fact, questions of value and questions of policy.

questions of fact

Questions of fact deal with what is true and what is false. 'Did Mr Jones steal money from the club's savings account?' is a question of fact. Jones either committed the crime or he did not. Questions of fact also describe existing conditions. For example, 'Where should the company locate the new staff cafeteria?' is a question of fact which describes a matter of place.

questions of value

Questions of value concern judgements of quality: whether something is good or bad, desirable or undesirable. 'How well do adult literacy programmes work?' is a question of value because it does not ask whether such programmes exist, but questions the quality of the programmes.

questions of policy

Questions of policy are enquiries into an action that might be taken in the future. Such questions often include the word 'should'. 'Should this student be suspended for cheating in an examination?' or 'Should the university build a new library?'

The type of question determines the purpose of the group and the nature of the information it requires. Of course, it may be necessary to discover facts and to clarify values before the group can decide on an action, but knowing the overall purpose helps to keep members on track in their discussion and guides them in the search for relevant information.

5.6.2 Analysing and researching the problem

Defining words and phrases

Before a group can discuss a problem or find a solution, all members must ascribe the same meaning to any word or phrase that may be ambiguous. For example, 'We need to raise a lot of money' or 'The company's internal mail service is too slow' or 'What should the department do about people who are not getting the job done?' can mean different things to different people. The members must agree on what exactly 'too slow' means, and how much 'a lot of money' is, or what 'not getting the job done' involves.

Seeking out information

The information that groups need to discuss a problem will vary. Sometimes relevant personal experience of group members is the most important source of information. Other problems can be investigated by direct observation.

For example, visually inspecting traffic conditions at a school crossing can tell you the specific nature of the problem. In the case of the late delivery of mail, personal interviews with the person in charge of the mail room and the messenger who delivers the mail may yield the necessary information. Information on the value of adult literacy programmes could be obtained from a library.

5.6.3 Deciding what the solution should accomplish

Most problems do not have a single solution. There are usually a number of alternatives. Before a group can arrive at a decision, it must establish realistic and acceptable criteria for what the solution should accomplish. For example, in evaluating alternatives, the mail committee might decide that any solution that does not get the mail to its destination twenty-four hours after it was received in the mail room is unacceptable.

5.6.4 Finding and evaluating solutions

Often a group can find many alternatives that may lead to a decision. Some of them will have to be discarded because they are impractical, others because they do not meet the criteria that have been set. One way of generating and evaluating solutions is to encourage the free flow of ideas

brainstorming

by brainstorming. **Brainstorming** encourages creative thinking as it requires that everyone states ideas as they come to mind, in random order, until a long list has been compiled. In ten to fifteen minutes of intensive concentration, you may think of several solutions to a problem yourself, but a group may come up with ten, twenty, thirty or more possible solutions in the same time. Brainstorming means that everyone temporarily suspends criticism and evaluation of ideas until the end of the session. If people feel free to make suggestions — even if they seem impractical or quite ridiculous at the time — they tend to think more creatively than if each idea is criticised as it is presented. Only after the brainstorming session is finished, is each solution evaluated as to its practicality and the degree to which it meets the criteria.

The one that meets the most criteria and is the most practical is usually selected.

5.6.5 Implementing the solution

The final step in a discussion is to offer suggestions about how the solution can be implemented. Sometimes the group itself has the power to initiate the solution; at other times, it conveys its proposals and suggestions to the person or people concerned. In the case of the mail problem, the group members would recommend a solution to the head of the mail room who (hopefully) agrees to try it for a month to see if it works. If, at the end of the month, the group finds that the plan is not working, it will have to meet again to consider different solutions.

5.7 Differences between interpersonal and group communication

We conclude this unit by pointing out that, while interpersonal and small-group communication both occur in a face-to-face situation, there are differences between them. Burton and Dimbleby (1995:225) have identified the differences as follows:

> In a one-to-one situation we are presenting our Self according to our self-concept and our perception of the other person(s) and the social context. When we are part of a group, however, the dynamics of the group, its tasks and social relationships mean that we are more conscious of playing a role and of being concerned with the *group*. The group, when it's working cohesively, develops a life of its own of which the individual members are merely a part — we subordinate our individual needs and motives for the sake of the group.

Case 5.1

A company which supplies computers to a variety of businesses in a large city in South Africa has received complaints from several of its customers that only white staff are sent to instal and service the computers. In response to these complaints, the company arranges for a task group to investigate whether affirmative action should be introduced in the company. During the first meeting, the leader of the task group asks for suggestions from the group members. Chaos ensues because each member of the group shouts out his or her ideas, opinions and solutions. Some of the suggestions and comments are totally impractical. Others are sound but, because most people have not had sufficient time to think about the problem before the meeting, even the best ideas are presented in a way that cannot easily be implemented. The leader asks for silence and then says: "Thank you for your enthusiasm and the variety of ideas being offered. However, if we are to reach a decision we need to thrash out all these ideas and come up with a workable solution that we can present to management. We are therefore going to follow a recognised problem-solving sequence. I will guide you as we go along."

After you have studied this case and thought about the situation, write down how you would implement the five stages in the problem-solving sequence described in section 5.6 above.

Summary

We began this unit by defining a small group and pointing out the advantages and disadvantages of working in small groups. We then explained that the characteristics of effective groups include having an optimum number of members, a good working environment, cohesiveness and commitment to the task, and a respect for group norms. We identified the types of roles that group members play as task roles and maintenance roles. This was followed by a discussion of the important role played by the leader of a group, as well as two theories about leadership: leadership traits and leadership styles. We also pointed out some guidelines for becoming an efficient leader. We then discussed different types of communication networks that operate in small groups and the consequences of each. The next part of the unit dealt with an investigation into the ways groups discuss the problems they have to address and the decisions that are made. We ended the unit with a short note on the differences between interpersonal and small-group communication.

Test-yourself

1 Select two groups to which you belong that you feel have an effective and an ineffective group climate. For each group, identify the types of behaviour exhibited by members. How did each climate affect your own participation in the group? How is each climate affected by your relationship with group members?

2 Choose a group of which you are a member and try to identify three group norms. Check your perception by asking other group members if they agree with your selection.

3 List three positive and three negative qualities you bring to groups. How could you overcome the negative qualities? Is your productivity in the group affected by your behaviour?

4 Try to determine the role that each member of a group to which you belong may be playing.

5 Choose a group of which you are a member and analyse which of the following had the greatest effect on group interaction: group size; group climate; presence or lack of cohesiveness; commitment to the task; adherence to norms. On what do you base your analysis?

6 Observe the leaders of the small groups to which you belong and classify each leadership style as democratic, autocratic or laissez-faire. Under which leadership style do you work best? Why?

7 What is your leadership style? What are its strengths and weaknesses?

8 Use the following list of questions to judge the success of the last discussion group of which you were a

member: (1) Did you feel comfortable in the group? (2) Did everyone participate and interact? (3) Were the group sessions enjoyable? (4) Did you find the task of the group enjoyable? (5) Was the topic adequately and efficiently covered? (Hybels & Weaver 1989:228).

Suggested reading

Barker, LL, Wahlers, KJ, Watson, KW & Kibler, RJ. 1991. *Groups in process: an introduction to small group communication.* 4th edition. Englewood Cliffs, NJ: Prentice-Hall.

Beebe, SA & Masterson, JT. 1994. *Communicating in small groups: principles and practices.* 4th edition. New York: HarperCollins.

Brilhart, JK & Galanes, GJ. 1989. *Effective group discussion.* 6th edition. Dubuque, Iowa: Wm C Brown.

Cohen, WA. 1990. *The art of the leader.* Englewood Cliffs, NJ: Prentice-Hall.

Fisher, D. 1981. *Communication in organizations.* New York: West Publishing Company.

Janis, I. 1972. Groupthink. *Psychology Today* (5):43–46; 74–76.

Johnson, DW & Johnson, FP. 1993. *Joining together: group theory and group skills.* 4th edition. Englewood Cliffs, NJ: Prentice-Hall.

Lustig, MW & Koester, J. 1993. *Intercultural competence: interpersonal communication across cultures.* New York: HarperCollins.

Whetten, DA & Cameron, KS. 1993. *Developing management skills: communicating supportively.* New York: HarperCollins.

Organisational communication

Overview

We are all part of at least one organisation — a family, church, university, hospital, business, and so on. Most of us are employed in some or other organisation, either in the public or private sector of society. Our daily interaction with others and our social activities almost always take place in the context of an organisation. Because organisations play such a significant role in modern society, the field of organisational communication has become important both as a theoretical and an applied field of study. In our study of organisational communication, we first focus on various theoretical aspects of the topic and then apply that knowledge to a practical situation. We begin by explaining the terms organisation and organisational communication and then briefly examine four theoretical approaches to organisational communication: the classical approach, the human relations approach, the human resources approach and the systems approach. To gain an understanding of how communication 'works' in an organisation, we examine the structure of communication in the organisation. Structure is concerned with the information channels, hierarchies and communication networks in the organisation. We pay attention to the four main functions of communication in the organisation and then end the unit with a case which is based on some aspects of communication that are relevant in a small private sector organisation such as a fast-food outlet.

Learning outcomes

At the end of this unit you should be able to do the following.

1 Define the following terms and provide an example of each based on your own experience of organisations: *organisations, organisational communication, bureaucracy, enterprise, voluntary organisation.*

2 Identify four theoretical approaches that can be used to study organisational communication. Briefly describe how each approach views the role of communication in the organisation.

3 Explain the purpose of *downward, upward* and *lateral communication* in the organisation, as well as the purpose of the *grapevine.*

4 Explain what is meant by *information channels, communication networks* and *hierarchies,* using examples based on your own experience of communication.

5 Explain four functions of organisational communication. Illustrate your answer with examples based on your own experience of organisations.

6 Apply the knowledge you have gained in this unit to your own participation in organisations.

7 Carry out the activities set for the case at the end of this unit.

Introduction

Communication has been called the life-blood of an organisation. Communication provides a basis for understanding virtually every human process that takes place in an organisation. Conflict and cooperation between organisational members, planning, morale, decision-making, leadership, authority, as well as the creation and maintenance of relationships, are all reflected in human interaction, or communication (Daniels & Spiker 1987). Especially in view of the changing nature of organisations in South Africa, the study of organisational communication has become particularly important in recent years.

We begin our study by defining *organisations* and *organisational communication.*

6.1 Organisations

Barker and Gaut (1996:200) define organisations as "collected groups of people that are constructed to achieve specific goals that could not be met by individuals acting alone". The definition makes several points. It tells us that organisations are deliberately established (constructed) for different purposes (to achieve specific goals). It also tells us that people in organisations are mutually dependent. Each member or group in the organisation contributes specific skills which together achieve the organisation's goals. Depending on their goals, organisations are loosely classified as bureaucracies, enterprises and voluntary organisations (Westrum & Samaha 1984).

bureaucracy

A *bureaucracy*, also called a public sector organisation, is a full-time, nonprofit organisation which is financed out of national, regional or local government taxes and provides an extensive range of services to the public. Examples of public service organisations include prisons, schools, government departments, hospitals and libraries.

enterprise/ business

In contrast, a private sector organisation such as an *enterprise* or *business* is a full-time organisation set up to make money for its owners by producing goods and services or by investing in other organisations. A bank, a factory and a restaurant are examples of enterprises.

voluntary associations

Voluntary associations are made up largely of members who do not have a full-time commitment to the organisation, and include churches, unions, clubs and political parties.

The above classification also serves to emphasise the relationship between organisations and society. An organisation can in fact be seen as a social structure which exists in a larger social environment (society) that is constantly changing. The organisation is extremely sensitive to influences in the environment and may, in turn, influence that environment. Those of you who work in an organisation, or who are associated with an organisation such as a school or government department, are probably well aware of how changing social circumstances in South

Africa have influenced the nature of almost every organisation in our society.

To maintain links with the environment, to adapt to changing circumstances, and to function rationally and efficiently, organisations require information. *Communication* is the critical element in the processing of information because information that does not reach its destination serves no purpose. We therefore turn to the question: what do we mean by the term *organisational communication*?

6.1.1   Organisational communication

Organisations are held together by communication. As soon as people gather together to begin organising, they need to make plans, arrive at decisions and settle disputes. Organisations depend on receiving, processing and transmitting information to achieve their **goals**. **Organisational communication** is an umbrella term for all the communication processes that occur in the context of an organisation. Organisational communication involves one-on-one communication (between a manager and an employee), small-group communication (meetings), public communication (public speeches by a chief executive officer) and mass communication (press releases, company newsletters, new product announcements).

organisational communication

Each of these forms of communication takes place both inside (internally) and outside (externally) an organisation. **Internal communication** refers to the messages that are shared among members of an organisation. Internal communication is usually concerned with work-related matters and provides the means for people to work together and cooperate with each other. An organisation, however, does not exist in isolation; it is an element in the structure of society and must adapt to social needs and changes in order to survive. An organisation may want to change its image in the community, for example, or advertise a new product. Organisations therefore establish **external communication** channels to gather information from the environment and to provide the environment with information about the organisation.

internal communication

external communication

6.2 Theoretical approaches to organisational communication

Infante, Rancer and Womack (1990) explain that, before the Industrial Revolution in England, most businesses were small, family-operated enterprises. The owner knew the employees well because they lived in the same community. After the increased mechanisation of the Industrial Revolution, manufacturing businesses grew much larger. With this expansion came the rise of a class of managers hired by the owner to make the business run smoothly. At the same time, theories were developed to explain how managers could perform their jobs more efficiently and effectively. The four most common approaches to organisational communication are the classical approach, the human relations approach, the human resources approach and the systems approach.

6.2.1 The classical approach

classical approach

The ***classical approach*** originated in the late nineteenth and early twentieth centuries when the assembly-line technologies that were developed for factories during the Industrial Revolution were applied to other types of organisations as well. Classical theory emphasises the importance of efficient management and high productivity. In this approach communication functions mainly to establish managerial control, provide workers with job instructions, and enable managers to gather information for planning. Most of the communication in the organisation flows from management to subordinates. There is also a sharp distinction between the private and work lives of employees. What happens at home is of no concern to management, even if it has an effect on the employee's work. It has been said that classical theory regards the organisation as a machine, and the people who work in it are merely cogs in the machine. The role of the individual is not very important because, like the parts of a machine, any worker can be removed and replaced without unduly disrupting the smooth running of the organisation.

Largely in reaction to the strict regulation and control of the classical school, the human relations school of organisational theory developed in the 1930s.

6.2.2 The human relations approach

An experiment conducted in the 1930s, known as the Hawthorne Studies (Roethlisberger & Dickson 1939), attempted to identify the ideal work environment to encourage high productivity, loyalty and motivation among employees. The researchers concentrated on the effects of lighting on worker output in the Hawthorne Electrical Company in the United States. They noticed that each time they adjusted the lights — whether they were made brighter or dimmer or practically turned off — worker productivity improved. They concluded that the increase in productivity was not due to changes in lighting at all — but to the attention workers were receiving. They suggested that workers should not be treated as cogs in a machine, but as individuals with personal needs and goals. Strategies should be developed to ensure congenial working conditions and to help employees fulfil their needs and goals. The researchers also stressed that the work environment includes interpersonal and social relationships among workers, as well as their formal work relationships. They recommended that the feelings and attitudes of workers, their grievances and personal goals cannot be ignored in the pursuit of efficiency. This line of

human relations approach

study is known as the ***human relations approach*** and stresses that organisational efficiency depends on strategies for increasing the work satisfaction and personal happiness of the individual employee. It also acknowledges the importance of social relations in organisational life — cliques or informal groups are a reality that affects the organisation. The contribution of this approach is that the importance of personal interaction between the formal system and its employees was established — organisations must provide upward channels of communication that enable employees to approach management. The human relations school has been accused of being a manipulative management strategy designed to increase worker output by pretending to be concerned about people, yet still treating them as cogs in the organisational machine. However, it provided the groundwork for future theories, such as the human resources approach.

6.2.3   The human resources approach

The **human resources** perspective of organisations developed in the late 1950s in response to the shortcomings of the human relations theory. According to this approach, workers are considered as sources of suggestions and ideas, and it is management's task to encourage people to contribute to the organisation in diverse ways and thereby to maximise productivity. The human resources approach particularly stresses participative decision-making and effective employer-employee relations because it maintains that workers are more motivated, productive and independent, and more satisfied with their work, when they are consulted about decisions that directly affect their work activities. In respect of communication, the human resources school emphasises genuine participation by all employees. Employees' ideas and suggestions are sought and encouraged and decision-making is not limited to higher management, but is encouraged at all levels of the organisation. Frequent communication is considered a necessity and management is expected to arrange group discussions, develop skilled group communication and leadership skills, and to motivate individuals towards the achievement of personal and organisational goals.

6.2.4   The systems approach

The **systems approach** regards the organisation as a whole (system) which is made up of separate parts, each of which has a relationship to all the other parts and to the environment in which the organisation exists. All the system parts are dependent on one another in the performance of organisational activities. Any change in one component inevitably affects the other system components. For example, should a factory introduce new equipment for the performance of quality control on its products, this will affect workers who were previously employed to perform the task manually. All the parts of the system must therefore coordinate their activities and functions to remain in a state of equilibrium or balance. For this purpose, relevant information is provided through efficient internal communication channels. For example, in a company that manufactures shoes, we might identify the sales department and the production department as two interrelated subsystems. If the sales department promises 200 pairs of shoes to customers and the production department makes only 100 pairs, then there will be problems in the organisation because it is out of balance. Through internal communication, the two departments can share relevant information and coordinate or integrate their activities.

Organisations also exchange information with their environment. External communication channels in the organisation must allow a free, open and rapid flow of information between the organisation and the society in which it exists. It is particularly important for the organisation to establish feedback channels to gather information that will allow it to adapt to needs and changes in the environment. An organisation that does not understand the needs of society will soon go out of existence. In the systems approach, communication is crucial to the organisation because it is the unifying element that allows the system to function efficiently, achieve its goals and remain in a state of balance.

Our discussion of the different approaches emphasises that organisations have different ways of coordinating the activities of the organisation and directing the way in which members of the organisation perform their tasks. In other words, there are different ways of managing the organisation. Communication plays a crucial role in determining how the organisation is managed. Different approaches to organisational communication directly affect the way communication travels in the organisation and how it is used in the organisation. In the next part of this unit, we examine the structure of communication in the organisation: who communicates with whom, how much information is received, and which channel is used.

6.3 Structure of organisational communication

Structure in this context refers to the components of the communication system in an organisation, most importantly the channels of communication through which information is sent and received. We begin by examining the formal and informal channels of communication in the organisation.

6.3.1 Formal and informal communication channels

You should be aware that a channel is the route by which a message or information travels. Channels of information in the organisation are described by distinguishing between the formal and informal flow of information. **Formal channels** are the official channels through which communication is exchanged. Formal channels may be written or oral and include personal instructions, interviews, training programmes, letters, memoranda and oral reports. However, information is also exchanged unofficially or **informally** during, for example, conversations among employees. Such information may be work-related or may be concerned with social and personal matters. Informal channels may at times prove to be a more effective means of communication than the organisation's formal channels.

formal/informal channels

6.3.2 Hierarchies

Information is distributed throughout an organisation in a hierarchical structure. The **hierarchical** structure of an organisation is often depicted in an organisational chart (illustrated in figure 6.1). As you can see, it is a linear diagram showing the status of different members of an organisation and the relationships among them. It is important to be aware of the hierarchical levels in an organisation, as the hierarchy affects the interpersonal relations of its employees and controls the channels of communication within the organisation. The hierarchy also controls the frequency and quality of daily interactions among people. To provide a practical example: should the president of a manufacturing company wish to convey a message about changes in the way goods are to be packed for delivery, he or she is unlikely to deliver the message directly to the packers. Instead he or she instructs the head of the packaging department who, in turn, conveys the information.

hierarchies

Figure 6.1: An organisational chart

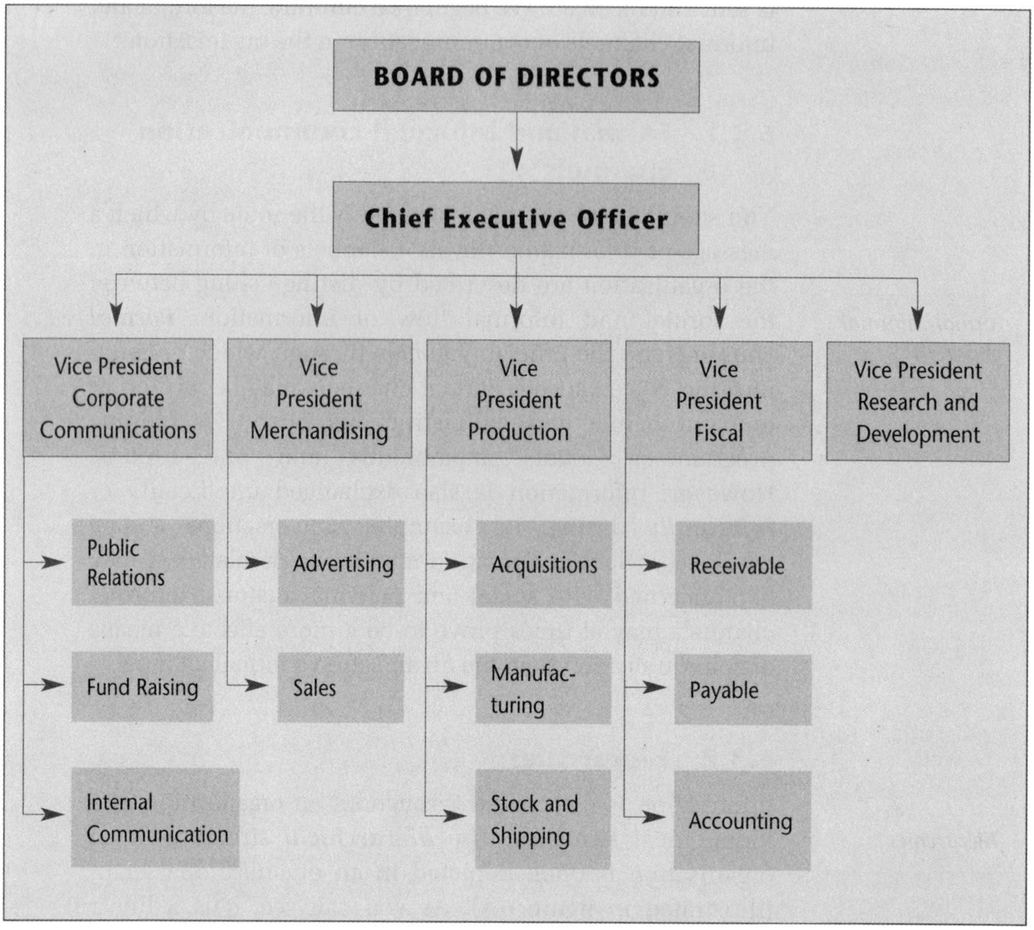

(Adapted from Phillips 1982:12)

6.3.3 Flow of information in the organisation

The flow of information refers to the direction in which messages travel in the organisation. In organisational communication, we generally talk about information that proceeds formally in vertical (upward and downward) and lateral (horizontal) directions, and about information that flows informally along the grapevine.

Downward communication

downward

Downward communication flows from top to bottom in the organisational hierarchy; that is, from those who hold positions with more authority to those with less authority, usually from superiors (management) to subordinates (employees). Downward messages are usually work-related and are disseminated through formal communication channels.

Messages sent from managers to employees have five purposes, namely to provide

1   specific instructions on how to do the work;

2   information which encourages an understanding of the task and its relationship to other organisational tasks and, in this way, supplies a rationale or reasons for the work;

3   information about organisational policies, procedures and practices;

4   feedback on performance to employees;

5   information regarding the organisation's orientation towards the goals of the organisation.

Upward communication

Sending messages is not the only concern in an organisation. Management also needs feedback on how a message has been received and acted upon. In addition, there are times when employees find it necessary to communicate information to someone in authority. *Upward* communication flows from subordinates to superiors and usually takes place via the same channels as downward communication.

upward

Lateral or horizontal communication

Lateral (or *horizontal*) communication describes communication between people on the same hierarchical level — that is, between employees of the same status — and may take the form of work-related messages, or may provide social interaction. The channels used for lateral communication are similar to those used for downward and upward communication.

lateral/ horizontal

In some organisations, the upward flow of messages is the source of communication problems, as employees often believe that the honest expression of their thoughts and feelings could cause them to get into trouble with management. Consequently, they only communicate what they think their superiors would like to hear. Many organisations today strive to create an open communication climate by implementing programmes to encourage upward and lateral communication.

The grapevine

grapevine

The **grapevine** is not prescribed by the organisation. It is an informal channel of information and its flow follows an unpredictable course both vertically (up and down) and laterally. It is used to spread rumours as well as to convey important information such as news on promotions, personnel changes, annual salary adjustments and organisational policy changes. As Pace (1983:57) points out, the metaphor is apt: "a grapevine seems to grow and send out shoots in all directions, capturing and hiding the fruit under a cover of heavy leaves, almost defying detection". Field research indicates that grapevine communication travels very quickly and is also reasonably accurate.

Grapevine communication is less heavily laden with task information than with information about people, attitudes, relationships, interpretations, predictions, values, norms and needs. The dysfunctional aspect of the grapevine is that it fosters and spreads rumours. Because rumour lacks facts that can be substantiated, it may be damaging when circulated and possibly acted upon. Usually characterised by prejudice, emotion, bias and partial truths, rumours arise in situations where there is ambiguity or uncertainty about issues in the organisation. In other words, an organisation with a strong grapevine could be experiencing problems with its formal communication channels and networks — organisation members are simply not receiving sufficient information through recognised channels.

In its friendly form, the grapevine serves as a uniting force when there is high interest, in new policies or innovations in procedures and personnel. A grapevine is also likely to occur in organisations where people work closely together, or where they interface with other sources of information about the organisation from outside (Myers & Myers 1982:138).

The trend today is to accept the existence of the grapevine as an inevitable fact of organisational life. Researchers maintain that by learning to use it to better effect, managers can build teamwork and company loyalty, increase motivation and job satisfaction, and ultimately improve performance (Andrews & Baird 1992:80).

Communication networks

networks

Apart from vertical and lateral communication channels, communication may also take place through communication **networks** in the organisation. On the most basic level, a network can be identified by establishing **who** communicates with **whom**, and who the **central figures** and the **peripheral figures** are in the communication process (refer to section 5.5 for a detailed discussion of communication networks). Awareness of the potential networks in an organisation provides insight into what type of information is likely to be received by which people. In a university, for instance, policy decisions made by the senate about course curricula will be networked among deans of faculties and department heads (central figures), but not among the rest of the university staff (peripheral figures).

6.4 Functions of organisational communication

Koehler, Anatol and Applbaum (1981) identify four main functions of organisational communication: *informative, regulatory, integrative* and *persuasive* functions. As we discuss these functions, think about the purposes they serve and/or the effects the functions have on people and activities in the organisation.

6.4.1 The informative function

informative

A crucial function of communication in the organisation is the provision of **information** to ensure its efficient operation. All members of the organisation require a constant flow of information to achieve organisation and individual goals. Both management and employees, for instance, need accurate, timely and well-organised information to enable them to do their work efficiently, make decisions, and resolve conflicts.

Kreps (1990) also emphasises the need for organisations to obtain information to adapt to changes in environmental conditions. Communication provides members with the information to exchange views on organisational activities, experiences, changes and plans. Most organisations have regular meetings during which information is exchanged about each area of the organisation, with a view to directing and coordinating behaviour toward implementing organisational changes.

6.4.2 The regulatory function

A second information-related function of organisational communication is to control and coordinate the activities of the organisation to ensure its successful operation. Manuals, policies, memoranda, rules and instructions collectively constitute a set of guidelines for the management of the organisation. **Regulatory** messages are work-oriented and have two main purposes:

regulatory

1   they inform employees about what tasks they are expected to perform in order to complete a specific assignment;

2   they inform employees about restrictions that are placed on their behaviour. Usually, managers send regulatory messages downward to employees, and expect compliance on the basis of their authority.

6.4.3 The integrative function

integrative

Closely related to the regulative function is the **integrative** function of organisational communication which is used to achieve organisational unity and cohesion. The integrative function is concerned largely with creating identity and uniformity in the organisation. As well as defining goals and tasks to facilitate the assimilation of new members, integrative messages are used to coordinate the work schedules of individuals, groups and departments, thereby eliminating wasted time and effort.

6.4.4   The persuasive function

persuasive

While information is essential to the functioning of an organisation, communication also **influences** members of an organisation. *Persuasion* can be used by both managers and employees. Managers, for instance, have found that power and the enforcement of authority do not always achieve the desired control over employees. They have discovered that persuasion is often more effective than authoritarian methods to gain employees' cooperation. Many successful managers realise that voluntary compliance on the part of employees often leads to more involvement than enforced compliance. Similarly, employees may use persuasion when, for instance, requesting an increase in salary.

To conclude this unit, we apply the theoretical knowledge that we have gained to the practice of communication in an organisation by studying a case based on a real situation.

Case 6.1

Thandi has seen an advertisement in the newspaper for a job as the manager of a take-away fish and chips shop in a new shopping complex. It is called *Fishies.* She applies for the job and is told to come for an interview. During the interview, the owner of the shop tells her that he owns several such outlets and emphasises that her role in the organisation will be primarily managerial because he does not have the time to manage the shop himself. There are six employees to prepare the food and clean the shop. Thandi will be responsible for setting goals, ordering supplies, arranging shifts, and training and motivating the employees. The manager also tells Thandi to keep abreast of happenings in the complex, such as shops that may be closing, and others that may be opening, especially fast-food outlets. He asks Thandi whether she has the skills to undertake the job. Thandi thinks about the course in organisational communication she has studied and immediately replies "Yes".

ORGANISATIONAL COMMUNICATION   **165**

After you have studied this case, answer the following questions.

1   What is *Fishies's* main goal?

2   Who is Thandi going to have to satisfy to achieve this goal? How do you think she can do this?

3   Thandi requires information to make decisions that will keep *Fishies* operating efficiently. Some of the information concerns the environment and comes from external sources. What sort of information would she look for and through which channels of communication would she expect to receive it?

4   How much attention should Thandi pay to information about happenings in the shopping complex that she receives through the grapevine?

5   Which channels and communication media would Thandi use to

▶   train her employees?

▶   motivate her employees?

▶   arrange shifts for her employees?

Summary

In this unit we first introduced the terms *organisations* and *organisational communication* to establish the meanings of these concepts in the context of communication studies. We then discussed some of the theories that have been developed to explain how managers in organisations can perform their jobs more efficiently and effectively. These theoretical approaches to organisational communication are the classical approach, the human relations approach, the human resources approach and the systems approach. Because it is important to gain an understanding of how communication 'works' in an organisation, we examined the structure of communication in the organisation by describing the information channels, hierarchies and communication networks in the organisation. Information channels can be formal or informal and information flows in different directions in the organisation: upwards, downwards, laterally and through the grapevine. The hierarchy is concerned with the status of different members of an organisation and the relationships among them, while communication networks describe who communicates with whom in the organisation. We also paid attention to the four main functions of communication in the organisation: the informative function, the regulatory function, the integrative function and the persuasive function. The unit ended with a case based on aspects of communication in a private sector organisation.

Test-yourself

1   Briefly describe how each of the four approaches to organisational communication that you have studied views the role of communication in the organisation.

2   Think of an organisation for which you have worked or with which you are familiar. Which approach to organisational communication seems to prevail? Provide examples to substantiate your point of view.

3   Explain the purpose of downward, upward and lateral communication in an organisation, using examples based on your own experience of organisations.

4   Consider an organisation with which you are familiar. What kind of communication is used the most: downward, upward or lateral? What communication problems or successes have resulted from the use of such types of communication?

5   Explain the term *grapevine* in two to three sentences. Then think about the type of information the grapevine in your organisation carries. What does this type of information reflect about the formal communication channels in the organisation?

6   Consider the following statement: 'Communication is the life-blood of any organisation'. Provide reasons for agreeing or not agreeing with the statement.

Suggested reading

Adelstein, ME & Sparrow, WK. 1990. *Business communications.* 2nd edition. Orlando, Fl: Harcourt, Brace, Javanovich.

Andrews, PH & Baird, JE. 1992. *Communication for business and the professions.* 5th edition. Dubuque, Iowa: Wm C Brown.

Blumberg, RL. 1987. *Organizations in contemporary society.* Englewood Cliffs, NJ: Prentice-Hall.

Corman, SR, Banks, SP, Bantz, CR & Mayer, ME (eds). 1990. *Foundations of organizational communication: a reader.* New York: Longman.

Goldhaber, GM. 1990. *Organizational communication.* 5th edition. Dubuque, Iowa: Wm C Brown.

Kreps, GL.1990. *Organizational communication: theory and practice.* 2nd edition. New York: Longman.

Rensburg, RS & Bredenkamp, C. 1993. *Aspects of business communication.* Cape Town: Juta.

Shockley-Zalabak, P. 1991. *Fundamentals of organizational communication: knowledge, sensitivity, skills, values.* New York: Longman.

7 Mass communication

Overview

In this unit we discuss the mass communication context. Mass communication has become an integral part of life in modern societies. We are living in the information age, an era when communication media and the technology associated with them have become central to nearly all that we do. We would be hard pressed to imagine a day in our professional or social lives without the mass media and mass communication. Yet there was a time when we did not have television or newspapers, and computers and cellular phones belonged in science fiction stories. In fact, there was a time when communication through speech was not possible because our prehistoric ancestors did not have our well-developed *language systems*. To fully understand the nature of communication, we need to have some idea of how it evolved and made possible the techniques and technologies that we refer to as 'communication' today. The history of communication also gives us insight into the way it influenced the development of civilisation and still exerts an influence on modern societies.

language system signs (words) and rules (grammar) of a language

In this unit we do not study the media used for mass communication (such as newspapers, television or computers) in great depth, but concentrate rather on the nature of mass communication and its effects on society and on people. We begin with a short history of the stages in human communication — how people have communicated over the ages. We then discuss modern mass communication. We first explain the term *mass* and define *mass communication* and *mass media* to distinguish between them. The process of mass communication is discussed by contrasting it with interpersonal communication. We follow this with the functions that mass communication performs in society.

In the remainder of the unit we broaden our understanding of mass communication and its influence on society and people by examining the components of the mass communication process in greater detail: the mass communicator, the mass medium and the audiences of mass communication. Throughout the discussion we refer to some of the research studies and theories that contribute to our understanding of this form of communication. We end the unit with a case study based on an advertisement for South African Airways.

Learning outcomes

At the end of this unit you should be able to do the following.

1   List the five ages in the history of communication in chronological order, name the medium or technological development that characterised each age, and describe the most important social outcome of each new development.

2   Define the terms *mass*, *mass communication* and *mass media*.

3   Describe the process of mass communication by contrasting interpersonal and mass communication.

4   Explain four functions of mass communication and illustrate each with an appropriate example.

5   Describe the role of the gatekeeper in mass communication and list some of the factors that influence the gatekeeper's choices.

6   Describe the effects of the mass media on public opinion by referring to the agenda-setting theory and the spiral of silence theory.

7   Describe how the magic-bullet theory, two-step flow theory, and uses and gratifications theory differ in explaining how the mass media influence their audiences.

8   Become a more critical recipient of mass communi-
    cation messages.

9   Answer the questions based on the case at the end of
    this unit.

Introduction

In your history lessons at school you probably learned
about the different stages in the development of the human
species, such as the Stone Age, the Bronze Age, the Iron
Age, and so on. These names refer to periods hundreds of
thousands of years ago during which ancient people made
tools from different materials, or developed ways for
solving their problems in producing food or making
weapons. Eventually human civilisation as we know it
would develop from these early inventions.

Another way of looking at human development is to define
a series of 'ages' in which our ancestors made advances in
their ability to communicate. It was equally important to
the development of civilisation to be able to exchange
information, record it, recover it, and disseminate (spread)
it. Communication enabled the inventions and solutions to
problems that marked the stages of human civilisation to be
shared and passed down to following generations (De Fleur
& Ball-Rokeach 1989).

Without some means of recording information, we would
not have been able to trace the development of civilisation.
An example of how knowledge of the past has been
acquired is provided by the cave paintings, dating from
25 000 to 10 000 years ago, which were discovered by
archaeologists in Spain, France and Southern Africa. The
paintings depict animals, geometric signs and human
figures that describe scenes of hunting and tribal rituals.
We do not know exactly what purpose they served at the
time, but their importance to us is that they are the oldest
surviving records of human communication. Today, we use
technological means to exchange, record, recover and
disseminate information. What is of interest to communication scholars is how techniques and technology that
made modern communication possible developed over the

ages. We ask questions such as the following: how did people communicate before speech and language? How did they record information? How did they transport it? What changes did the mass media and technology make in society and in the life of the individual?

7.1 A brief history of human communication

The following account of the history of communication is based on discussions in Schramm (1988), De Fleur and Ball-Rokeach (1989), DeFleur (1994) and Fang (1997).

The stages in human communication are associated with the development of speaking, writing, printing, and the mass media (newspapers, radio, film and television). The most recent stage is the information age, the outcome of the development of computer technology. As we discuss each of these stages, you should be aware that each successive communication development did not replace that which preceded it. Rather, it gradually built on what was already there. Our ancestors first learned to communicate by means of signals, and we still use them today (for example, waving your hand to greet someone). Then speech and language were added, followed by writing and mass communication. Today, we use all of these means of communication in addition to the rapidly spreading use of computers.

Another point to bear in mind is that the developments we discuss cannot be measured in terms of, say, hundreds of years. They cover a period of more than 500 000 years. The time span between speech and the invention of writing, and between writing and the invention of print, for example, was thousands of years, a concept difficult to convey in a short account such as this. The consequence is that there are necessarily many gaps in our 'story'. We have selected what we consider to be the most significant highlights in the history of communication.

The story of human communication begins some half a million years ago with small groups of prehistoric hunters who lived in caves. These people did not walk upright and were physically incapable of producing speech. They could produce vocal sounds, but their voice boxes had not yet developed sufficiently to generate and control the intricate sounds of speech. Although we have no records, scientists assume that their communication was similar to animal communication — that is, prehistoric people received and exchanged information about the environment (for instance, the presence of danger or food) through their senses: sight, smell, taste, touch and hearing. They also communicated with each other through gestures, posture and facial expressions, and expressed a limited number of sounds such as grunts and cries. Over time, people began to move out of the caves and settle in small communities. The need to communicate played an increasingly important role in their ability to participate in community life. The development of speech and language was the first major revolution in the means of communication available to human beings.

7.1.1   The age of speech and language

speech and language

Scientists estimate that **speech and language** originated some 40 000 years ago among people who had evolved to physically resemble human beings today. Not much is known about the origins of speech. One view is that it was a divine gift. Another view assumes that, as the human speech organs developed, recognisable words gradually developed from the basic sounds emitted by prehistoric people, and speech and language evolved. What is important is that speech gave people the ability to think and plan, to hunt and defend themselves more effectively, to invent ways of preserving food and keeping warm in winter, and to learn to cultivate the land. It was during this era that people also began expressing their creativity in the form of art — the cave paintings that have been discovered in different parts of the world. The development of speech and language thus had consequences for both individuals and society. While the ability to use language did not **cause** great changes, it made possible the transition from a hunting way of life to an agricultural way of life.

Some of the earliest agricultural communities settled along the fertile banks of the Tigris and Euphrates Rivers, the shores of the Mediterranean, and the banks of the Nile River. As these agricultural areas grew and developed over the centuries, people needed to find ways to record such matters as boundaries and land ownership. And, as their towns grew in size and commercial activities and trading increased, they also needed to keep records of buying and selling, and other transactions. It was needs such as these that prompted the invention of writing in about 3 500 BC.

7.1.2   The age of writing

The cave paintings produced by prehistoric people mentioned in section 7.1.1 are humanity's earliest attempts to record ideas in **graphic** form. They clearly depict animals, people and hunting scenes. However, we do not understand the purposes for which they were used and the meanings they held for the people who made them. Only the original artists could answer such questions accurately. What is important is that cave paintings provided people with a way of recording customs, traditions and ceremonies for succeeding generations that was more accurate than using the spoken word alone. For this reason, scientists regard cave paintings as the precursor to writing. The significant point about writing is that it enabled people to standardise and share the meanings of signs (words) because each language system has its own set of rules (such as grammar) to which everyone conforms.

The earliest forms of writing were **cuneiform** and **hieroglyphics**. Although the invention of writing allowed people to record and store information, the problem with hieroglyphics and cuneiform was that clay tablets and stone 'documents' were difficult to transport. The first advances towards a more portable writing medium were made by the Egyptians who invented the **papyrus**-making process in about 2 500 BC. Later, animal skins and **parchment** replaced papyrus, and paper (made from wood pulp) was finally invented by the Chinese in about AD 100.

The importance of light and portable media is that it provided the conditions for far-reaching social and cultural changes. Of prime importance is that it was no longer

writing

graphic
in the form of pictures

cuneiform
ancient system of writing with wedge-shaped characters on clay tablets

hieroglyphics
ancient Egyptian writing using picture symbols carved into stone

papyrus
a kind of paper made from water plants

parchment
a kind of paper made from animal skins

necessary to rely on the human memory to retain information and to pass the **culture** of a society to following generations by word of mouth. In Egypt, for example, papyrus was used to record the affairs of government, and to write down legal, literary, scientific, medical and religious ideas. Libraries were opened, and schools were established to teach a class of clerks, known as scribes, to write. It took many centuries, however, before the majority of people could read and write. In fact, it was not until the invention of printing in the fifteenth century that literacy started to spread.

culture
language, traditions, art, rituals and life-styles in a particular society

7.1.3   The age of print

print

The printing process is traditionally attributed to the invention of movable metal type by Johan Gutenberg of Mainz in Germany in 1450. Prior to this time, manuscripts and books were produced by craftsmen and monks who copied and recopied them by hand — a slow, laborious and expensive process. Gutenberg's invention revolutionised book production. The printing press spread rapidly throughout the world and by the beginning of the sixteenth century thousands of books were being produced. The importance of Gutenberg's invention is that it permitted the storage of large amounts of information. Printing is said to have marked the start of the modern world because it changed the way information was conveyed and, for the first time, literacy came within reach of the masses. DeFleur (1994) makes the important point that the new medium of communication did not displace earlier ways of communication. Then and now, spoken language remains the primary mode of communication. Writing, and then printing, supplemented oral communication, but never replaced it.

As techniques were developed for more rapid printing and improved road and postal systems made distribution easier, **news-sheets** — an early form of newspaper — began to flourish and their circulation increased rapidly. While the early news-sheets of the seventeenth and eighteenth centuries were aimed at the educated elite, the mass newspapers of the nineteenth and twentienth centuries

news-sheet
a one-page newspaper

were designed to appeal to the growing numbers of literate artisans and merchants in the rapidly developing urban-industrial cities of England, Europe and America (refer back to section 1.4.2 where we discussed the Industrial Revolution).

social significance
how society was influenced or changed

The *social significance* of printing is that with the spread of books, information became available to a greater number of people. For the first time in history, they were able to share knowledge that had previously been denied to them. As more and more people learned to read and write, their thinking was freed from the restrictions of church and government. New political and religious ideas began to circulate in society and, throughout Europe and America, revolutionary movements emerged, making use of print to disseminate their ideas to increasingly receptive publics. Particularly with the spread of newspapers, public opinion became something that political leaders had to take into account. Although it came after book production, the great success and wide distribution of the newspaper made it the first true mass communication medium.

7.1.4 The age of the electronic mass media

electronic mass media

Scientific discoveries and technological inventions during the nineteenth century (such as electricity and the telegraph), laid the foundations that would eventually lead to mass electronic media. Towards the end of the nineteenth century people were able to send telegrams and cables, and talk to each other on the telephone. It is important to note that the advent of electricity created the 'wired world' and, for the first time in history, it became possible to separate communication and transportation. Until then, the medium which carried the information had to be physically transported from one place to another. Books and newspapers had to move from place to place in much the same way as clay tablets in ancient times. Information travelled only as fast as the messenger who carried it. With the invention of the telegraph and the telephone, information could be **transmitted** rather than transported. Communication over vast distances was no longer dependent on the available means of transportation. The effects of this 'revolution' are still in evidence today. The fax machine, for example, can transmit a letter speedily without the need for mail delivery. It is also important to note that, while the telegraph facilitated the sending of information that could be collected at a distance for later use, the telephone was an immediately interactive medium (Crowley & Heyer 1991). In other words, there was no longer a time delay between the transmission of information and its reception by the person to whom it was addressed.

Radio

radio

Towards the close of the nineteenth century Marconi invented the first 'wireless telegraph' which permitted signals to be transmitted without the use of electric wires. By Christmas of 1906, a Canadian professor, Reginald Fessenden, was able to broadcast a musical programme from his experimental laboratory in Massachusetts. In 1908, another American inventor, Lee de Forest, demonstrated the transmission of the human voice from the Eiffel Tower in Paris, and the signals were picked up by radio operators some 500 miles away. Technological inventions and public interest in the possibilities of using radio for commercial purposes followed, and by 1912 the first licensed radio station transmitting news and music was operating in California. After the end of the First World War the idea of using radio to broadcast messages to large audiences emerged, and by 1928 a number of commercial networks were operating across the United States of America.

The British Broadcasting Corporation was established in 1922 and similar developments took place in other industrialised countries. By the 1930s radio achieved a central position as a mass medium providing news and entertainment to an increasing number of audiences. During the Second World War radio was the primary means for keeping people informed on the progress of the war.

Film

film

The invention of photography and developments in optics and chemistry in the late nineteenth century made it possible to record images on film. In 1895 the first projected images (ten short films that lasted about 20 minutes) were demonstrated in France by the Lumière Brothers. By the early twentieth century the movie camera and projector were available and motion pictures became an important means of providing entertainment. The early films were offered as an attraction at fairgrounds but, from 1905, permanent cinemas were being built in Europe and the United States. The most important person associated with the first full-length (silent) movies was David Wark Griffith, an American film-maker who directed films such as *The birth of a nation* (1915) and *Intolerance* (1916) which are still regarded as classics today. The first sound film, *The jazz singer*, was made in 1927 and colour was widely used in films from the 1950s. Since then, increasingly sophisticated technology has created the type of films we as audiences have come to expect when we visit the cinema.

The golden age of film in the United States was from 1930 to the late 1940s during which time thousands of films were made. The content of most of these films was sufficiently bland to provide excellent and inexpensive family entertainment, especially during the **Depression**. While the majority of films still seek to amuse or entertain by providing diversion and entertainment, films are socially significant in other ways. For example, many documentaries seek to educate people and most propaganda films have a persuasive influence. The majority of films reflect the society that produces them and thereby enrich our cultural experiences as well. Botha (1997) argues that, while film is an important part of any country's culture, this is particularly true in a country like South Africa, where film can make an important contribution to the democratisation and development that need to take place. For example, a film such as *Taxi to Soweto* explores some of the changes taking place in South African society in a humorous way that nevertheless helps people to make sense of what is happening around them. However, in the

depression
the world-wide economic depression of the early 1930s

past, apartheid policy and ineffective subsidy structures contributed to the fragmentation of the South African film industry so that, for most of its history, it has reflected apartheid ideology and ignored socio-political turmoil as well as the realities experienced by black South Africans (Botha 1997).

Television

television

Developments in film and radio prompted attempts to transmit images and sound over the air, and so television was born. Television was demonstrated in London in 1926 and, as early as 1936, the British Broadcasting Corporation offered a regular daily broadcast. In the United States, television began operating in 1940. However, its growth was halted by the outbreak of the Second World War, and it was not until the 1950s that development started again. The expansion of television was rapid. For example, in 1950, there were only about one million television sets in American homes. Within ten years their number rose to about sixty million, while less than twenty years later television was being used in approximately 90 per cent of American homes (Schramm 1988). Note that the discussion about the social significance of film is relevant to television as well. In most societies, even though it may be primarily used for entertainment and information (for example news and discussion programmes), television is also part of the culture of the society.

The mass media are so deeply embedded in modern society that we cannot imagine life without them. Not only would we be deprived of the source of much of our entertainment, but the incredible flow of information that we accept as 'natural' would not be available. A significant social outcome of developments in the mass media is that the **increase in the speed** of communication and the increase in the volume (amount) of communication and information brought about changes that created the information society (discussed below). Equally significant is what Fang (1997:138) describes as the creation of the *"Communication Toolshed Home"* which has transformed the average person's home into the

Communication Toolshed Home

central location for receiving information and entertainment. The Communication Toolshed Home is equipped with 'tools' such as radio, television, video cassette recorders (VCRs), compact discs (CDs), newspapers, books, magazines, fax machines and computers, all of which perform a variety of communication functions that make it unnecessary to leave the home in order to obtain entertainment and information.

7.1.5 The information age

information age

Scientists agree that we are in the midst of a new stage in the development of communication: the *information age*, also called the computer age. There is no clear-cut distinction between the age of mass media and the information age — the information age is the inevitable outcome of the new technologies of the second half of the twentieth century. The significance of the information age is that it has created 'information societies', societies that depend for their economic survival on immediate access to large amounts of information on a global scale.

We can trace the beginnings of global communication — the world-wide network of communication — to the introduction of the computer and satellite technology after the Second World War. In 1945, a futurist writer, Arthur C Clarke, predicted that three satellites positioned in orbit over the earth could provide a global network for communication. By 1962, the first satellite, the *Telstar*, was in orbit around the earth. Today, more than forty satellites orbit the world. Most of the satellites are used for broadcast services — that is, television and radio signals are sent up to the satellite and are then relayed to different stations all over the world. Important news events happening in one country can be broadcast around the world via satellite as they are happening and are seen simultaneously by millions of people in many countries.

While the invention of the printing press made possible the sharing of large amounts of information on a massive scale, computer technology has made this process even more efficient. Computers are basically machines capable of processing and storing information. Originally used in large organisations to perform complicated mathematical calculations and to aid administration, they are used today in industry, medical research, the military, and the exploration of outer space, to name but a few examples. Computers are the basis of the **Internet**, the world-wide network that carries information and entertainment along what has become known as the *Information Highway*. Fang (1997) remarks that while scientists are yet to find a satisfactory definition of the Internet, it is not difficult to explain how it works. A person using a computer connected via a telephone to another computer anywhere in the world can send and receive large amounts of information on almost any imaginable topic along the Information Highway. Being connected to the Internet allows you to find out, for instance, the latest cricket score in a match being played in Australia, what courses are offered at Unisa, stock exchange prices in New York, or weather conditions in Paris.

> *Information Highway*
> imaginary high-way (network) that carries information and entertainment (the Internet)

In contrast to the thousands of years that elapsed between the development of speech and language, writing, and finally print, the most remarkable achievement of the twentieth century has been the speed with which communication developments have occurred. However, today's media still perform the same functions as the clay tablets and hieroglyphics of centuries ago — they move information across time and space. The difference is that information reaches unlimited numbers of people over vast distances at breathtaking speeds using incredibly sophisticated technology.

7.2 The concept 'mass'

> *mass*

The word **mass** itself has acquired positive and negative connotations in society and therefore influences the way people define and think about mass communication and the mass media. For example, *mass* can be used negatively to describe a mob of unruly and ignorant people. Therefore, it is not uncommon for people who think of mass in such derogatory terms to regard the mass media as being inferior and corruptive. In a more positive sense, *mass* is used to describe the strength and solidarity of ordinary people. It appears, for example, in terms such as 'mass movement', 'mass action' and 'mass support' (McQuail 1987). From such a positive perspective, the mass media are considered to be instruments of enlightenment for the majority of people. For our purpose, we pay attention to the neutral and descriptive meanings of the term. From such a perspective, *mass* has the following meanings:

▶ *mass* refers to the multiple or mass production of messages;

▶ *mass* refers to the large size of the audiences that are reached by the mass media;

▶ *mass* refers to an amorphous group of which the individual components are not readily distinguishable from each other (McQuail 1987).

mass communication

mass media

These meanings can be used to define and distinguish mass communication and mass media. **Mass communication** is a process of delivering information, ideas and attitudes to a sizeable and diversified audience through a medium developed for that purpose (Agee, Ault & Emery 1988). The **mass media** are the technologies and social institutions (such as newspapers, radio and television) that are involved in the production and distribution of messages to large audiences. It is important to be aware that, while the mass media are essential in the process of mass communication, they represent the technological instruments used to convey messages to large audiences; they do not constitute the process involved.

7.3   The process of mass communication

It is perhaps easier to understand the process of mass communication by first contrasting it with something we are already familiar with — interpersonal communication — and then illustrating its complex nature with the help of a model.

In unit 1 we described interpersonal communication as a transactional process between two (or more) people in a face-to-face encounter. Interpersonal communication usually involves a single source (the communicator) and a single receiver (the recipient) who are known to each other and whose purpose it is to engage in a meaningful exchange of messages. A characteristic of interpersonal communication is that the participants continually provide feedback or respond to each other's verbal and nonverbal messages. Feedback is immediate and gives communication its dynamic nature by allowing the participants to exchange roles while negotiating meaning to reach mutual understanding.

Mass communication has distinctive characteristics which concern the basic components in the communication process. As we discuss these characteristics, bear in mind that, unlike interpersonal communication, mass communication is **mediated** — it involves the use of complex technology to multiply messages and transmit them to large numbers of recipients simultaneously. The term used to describe the recipients of mass communication is the *mass audience*.

mediated

The **communicator** in mass communication is not a single individual, but a member of a team within an organisation (such as a newspaper or television station) involved in the production and distribution of messages. On a newspaper, for example, one finds (amongst others) reporters, editors, photographers, layout artists, printers and salespeople, each of whom contributes to the production and distribution of the newspaper. Similarly, the **recipients** of mass communication are not single individuals but consist of large audiences who are not personally known to the communicator, or even to each other. The audience is too large for the communicator to be able to interact with personally. Because the demographic characteristics of audience members are diverse, **messages** are not personally addressed to particular individuals, but are public — they are directed at groups of people who may not have very much in common.

mass communicator

mass recipients

mass messages

There is also little or no interaction or **feedback** from the audience back to the communicator because the audience

feedback

mass medium

members are unable to use the same *medium* to reply to the communicator. Their access to the mass media is restricted by the media organisation and the complex technology involved means that the majority of people do not have the specialised skills required to **encode** their messages in a mass medium. The recipients may still provide feedback by, for example, telephoning or writing a letter to the media organisation, but such feedback is not immediate — it is delayed. Because of the time lapse, the free passage of messages that characterises face-to-face communication is lacking in mass communication.

The conclusion is reached that the mediated messages of mass communication set it apart from interpersonal and small-group communication, and even public speaking, which all occur in face-to-face situations. Consequently, mass communication has been described as an encounter with a **medium** and a **message** rather than a **relationship with another person**, as in interpersonal communication.

7.3.1 A model of mass communication

We turn now to a model (figure 7.1) which highlights this difference in its depiction of the process of mass communication.

The model illustrates and helps to explain the sequence of events in mass communication as well as the relationship between the basic components of the process: communicator, medium, message, audience and feedback. The model clearly shows that the media organisation occupies an intermediary position between the communicator on the one hand and the audience on the other (McQuail & Windahl 1981).

In the model, A is the communicator (such as a politician or an advertiser) who would like to transmit a message (represented as X') to a mass audience (B) about a certain thing or event (X_1, X_2, X_3, X_4). But A cannot reach the audience directly. He must first address his message to the mass media organisation (C) which encodes and transmits

Figure 7.1: A model of mass communication

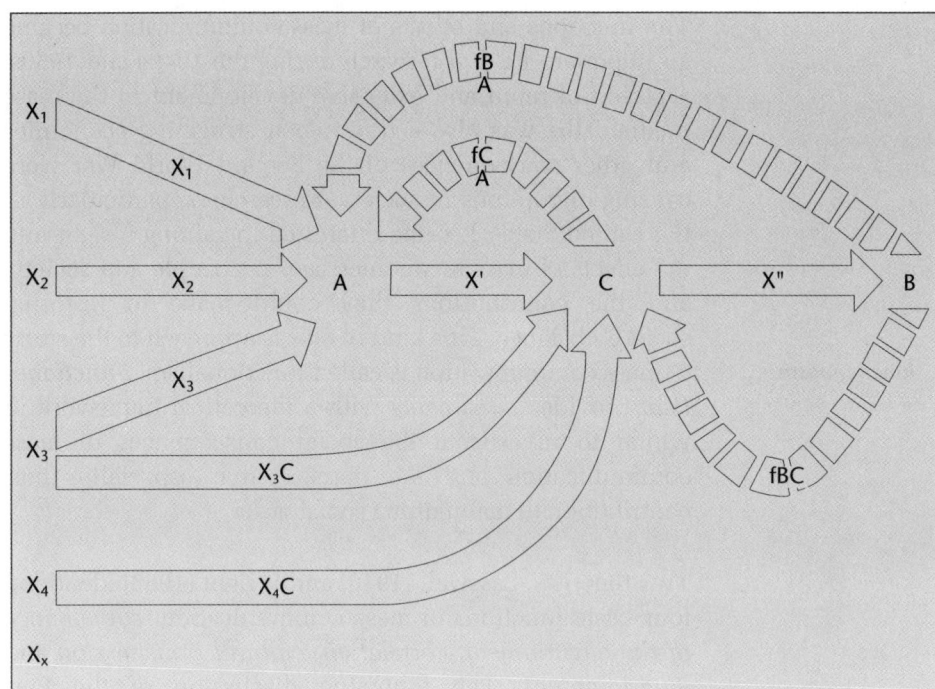

(Adapted from Westley & MacLean 1957 by McQuail & Windahl 1981)

the message (X") to the audience. A, the original source of the message, loses his position as the communicator. The media organisation takes over the communicative function. The audience encounters the messages of the media and not the original source of the message. A similar process occurs should members of the audience want to provide feedback (fBA) to the original communicator. Because they cannot reach A directly, the recipients may telephone or write to the media organisation (fBC) and the organisation relays the feedback (fCA) to the communicator.

The ability of mass communication to multiply messages and transmit them rapidly to large audiences has stimulated a considerable amount of investigation by communication researchers into the functions that mass communication performs in society.

7.4   Functions of mass communication

The functions and effects of mass communication became an important field of research during the 1940s and 1950s, a period of rapid and extensive development in the mass media. This was also a time when struggling economies and other consequences of the Second World War were causing disruptions in society. Researchers, particularly in the United States, became interested in gaining insight into the effects of mass media messages on people and society, and the contributions they could make to restoring society's balance. This kind of effects approach to the study of mass communication is called functionalism. **Functionalism** provides researchers with a theoretical framework in which to investigate the social consequences of mass communication and the mass media, especially their contribution to maintaining social order.

functionalism

Two theorists, Lasswell (1948) and Wright (1960) identified four basic functions of mass communication: *surveillance of the environment, correlation, cultural transmission* and *entertainment*. The following discussion of the four functions is based mainly on insights provided by Infante, Rancer and Womack (1990).

7.4.1   Surveillance of the environment

surveillance

The first function, **surveillance of the environment**, is considered the information and news-providing function of mass communication. The media keep us informed about national and international news ranging from world stock-market prices and revolutionary uprisings to local traffic and weather conditions. In times of crisis (a national drought, for example) one of the surveillance functions of the media is to inform people what is expected of them, thereby minimising confusion and contributing to social order.

7.4.2   Correlation

correlation

Closely linked to surveillance is the **correlation** function which deals with how the mass media select and interpret information about the environment. Articles in newspapers, or discussions on radio and television about political, economic or social events, for example, have been selected and interpreted by the mass media, and have consequences for the way we understand and respond to these events. Our attitudes and opinions about political figures, for instance, are often influenced by the impressions we receive from the mass media. A negative impression of the African National Congress, for instance, was reinforced for many years by the South African Broadcasting Corporation which continually portrayed it as a terrorist movement. On the other hand, public response to a television programme about the work done by *Operation Hunger* helped to gather funds for the organisation's work in feeding the hungry.

7.4.3 Cultural transmission

cultural transmission

The third function, **cultural transmission**, refers to the media's ability to communicate norms, rules and values of a society. Cultural transmission is a teaching function of mass communication. Television shows such as *Family Ties* and the *Bill Cosby Show* have been mentioned as programmes which promote values such as respect for authority and family harmony. Many children's programmes are designed to encourage behaviours which are considered appropriate in a given society.

7.4.4 Entertainment

entertainment

The fourth function of the mass media, **entertainment**, refers to the media's ability to present messages which provide escapism and relaxation. Although the entertainment function of the media has frequently been criticised because of the low quality content of some programmes, many current theorists recognise its positive consequences. They point out that mass communication provides relief from boredom, stimulates our emotions, helps fill our leisure time, keeps us company, and exposes us to experiences and events that we could not attend in person (Infante, Rancer & Womack 1990).

The functionalist approach is still used today to study the relationship between mass communication and society. It offers researchers a theoretical framework for examining the social consequences of mass communication, especially its contribution to the maintenance of social order. With regard to change in society, however, functionalism can only accommodate slow-moving, evolutionary change. It is incapable of accounting for sudden and fundamental change. Its application is thus limited to areas such as policy research, planning and evaluation. Functionalism has also been criticised by many theorists because it offers a limited view of communication. By concentrating on the functions that mass communication performs for society, it tends to overlook the **human** nature of communication and the fact that people construct **meaning** from messages. It has also been accused of having a conservative bias which justifies the maintenance of the existing social order and prevents any meaningful change from taking place.

The basic knowledge that you have gained thus far of the process of mass communication and its functions provides the context in which we study the mass communicator, the mass medium, and the audiences of mass communication in greater detail. As you study the remainder of this unit, you should bear in mind that the theories we discuss were developed to meet specific concerns about mass communication. As the mass media grew in popularity during the twentieth century, researchers began to show an interest in how these new forms of communication were influencing their audiences. Until the 1950s, research was concentrated on newspapers, film and radio. By the end of the 1950s, when television became widely available, people grew increasingly alarmed about what this new medium was doing to them and their society, and especially what it was doing to their children. Extensive studies have been carried out in connection with the effects of television viewing on children, but we do not discuss them here. Rather, we concern ourselves with theories that deal with the social effects of mass communication in a more general way. We have selected theories that examine the mass communicator, the mass medium and mass audiences. We begin with the mass communicator.

7.5   The mass communicator

We said earlier that the mass communicator is usually a member of a team within an organisation involved in the production and distribution of messages. Each member of the team has a particular function to fulfil. It has been suggested that one of the primary functions of the mass communicator is that of **gatekeeping**. A **gatekeeper** refers to an individual within an organisation who has the power to select and reject messages, and even to interpret and change them, thereby influencing the information received by a recipient or group of recipients (Tubbs & Moss 1991; Dimbleby & Burton 1992).

gatekeeper

To understand the definition as well as the role of the gatekeeper, think about the newspaper you may read every day. All major newspaper organisations are flooded with news stories that reach them daily from sources all over the world. The items that you read have been **selected** and put together by media personnel (editors) who decide which items are the most relevant. The control exercised by such editors in their gatekeeping role is that what has been left out may be as important to some readers as what has been included. Gatekeeping is a necessary aspect of mass communication, and is not limited to newspapers. Gatekeepers exist in all mass media organisations including radio, television and film. For example, the producer of a half-hour television documentary can include only a limited amount of the many hours of material that may have been videotaped for the programme. Similarly, the compiler of a women's weekly radio magazine programme may have to discard some of the items that were gathered in the course of the week because of the limitations of time. The choices made by the gatekeeper concerning which information to discard, and which to select and edit, are influenced by other variables as well (Tubbs & Moss 1991; Dimbleby & Burton 1992).

selection

A major consideration in the selection and rejection of media material is **economics**. The mass media are very expensive to operate and most media organisations have to show a profit to maintain themselves. One of their chief sources of income comes from the advertisers who pay

economics

heavily for media space and time, and expect to see results on their investment. A magazine advertisement for toothpaste, for example, sells not only because of the persuasive element in the advertisement, but as a result of the content in the rest of the magazine. The magazine editor tends to select material which will please the advertisers; that is, material which will appeal to the type of audiences the advertisers are aiming at.

news values

A second major source of income comes from the **audiences** who, for example, buy newspapers or magazines, or pay to watch a film in a cinema. To attract and satisfy large audiences, media personnel have to decide on both the news value and relevance of a particular story. *News values* (also called *newsworthiness*) are beliefs about what topics make good news, and can vary from one organisation to the next. Generally, stories that involve well-known personalities are considered to have more news value than stories about lesser known people. Likewise, stories which portray drama, such as children being rescued from a fire, or conflict between opposing parties, are often chosen in preference to stories which portray 'ordinary' events. The **relevance** of a particular programme is determined by deciding, for example, whether a story about striking miners in England or a radio drama set in Alaska will interest South African audiences.

policy and ideology

A major influence on the choices made by the gatekeeper is the *policy and ideology* of the media organisation. Policy refers to the criteria for news value laid down by a particular organisation, while ideology refers to the fact that most media organisations, especially newspapers, adopt a particular political point of view which is reinforced in their interpretation of news stories. You have probably noticed that, while they may cover the same events, three different newspapers interpret those events to coincide with their respective points of view. What you read in your newspaper is not an 'objective' report of the 'facts' but an interpretation of what has occurred. An organisation such as the South African Broadcasting Corporation (SABC), which broadcasts public service programmes, is expected to be impartial in its news reporting. Until 1994, the SABC was criticised for supporting Nationalist government policy in its selection and interpretation of political news events, thereby directing the perceptions of its viewers in a particular direction.

legal restrictions

ethics

Legal restrictions and *ethics* also influence the choices made by media organisations. Every country has legal restrictions on the type of messages the mass media may communicate. The media will generally avoid reporting malicious gossip about people, unless it is verifiable, for fear of being taken to court. Most organisations also follow a code of ethics in the interests of good taste. There are exceptions, of course, but most newspapers would probably decide not to publish photographs of mutilated bodies in an accident because it may offend some readers. Likewise, the majority of television stations would not broadcast pornographic material in the early evening when children might be watching.

7.6   The mass medium

We mentioned in our discussion of the functions of mass communication that, as mass communication became an increasingly prevalent form of communication, a great deal of research was (and is still) conducted on the effects of the mass media and their messages on society. An influential theory in this regard is the agenda-setting theory which gained prominence during the 1960s and 1970s.

7.6.1   Agenda-setting theory

public opinion

Agenda-setting refers to the way the mass media create public awareness and concern about important issues, thereby contributing to the shaping of public opinion. The concept of *public opinion* represents ideas about social issues (such as political elections) that are expressed and debated in public, and the opinions of the general public as a group, rather than of individuals. The underlying argument of agenda-setting is that the public responds, not to actual events in the environment, but to "pictures in our heads" that are created by the media in their reporting of news stories (Heath & Bryant 1992:281).

Agenda-setting is an extension of the gatekeeping function we discussed earlier, in that it is concerned with the selection of news stories and the prominence given to the stories by the media. The theory proposes that, in the same way that people set an agenda for important matters that require attention, the mass media select topics, issues and individuals they consider to be important and bring them to the attention of the public. The matters that the media choose to publicise ultimately become those that we think about and talk about. According to the theory, we think these matters are important because of the *media attention* they have received, regardless of how important they may really be. The result of highlighting an issue is that it is placed on the public agenda for serious discussion (Agee *et al* 1988; Infante, Rancer & Womack 1990). An example of agenda-setting is provided by Severin and Tankard (1988) who describe how New York newspapers 'created' a crime wave in the 1930s. There were always lots of crime stories that the press did not report. On one occasion, a reporter wrote up one of these stories because it involved a well-known family. A rival newspaper promptly looked for, and reported on, another crime. Soon, all the New York newspapers were 'finding' crimes to keep up with the others. The sudden increase in crimes reported in the press was perceived as a 'crime wave' by the public and, for a time, crime became the most discussed issue in New York. Although the crime rate had not actually risen, the public came to see crime as an important issue simply as a result of the media attention it received.

media attention

A conclusion about agenda-setting reached by many theorists was first expressed by Cohen in 1963: "The press may not be successful much of the time in telling people what to think, but it is stunningly successful in telling its readers what to think **about**" (Agee *et al* 1988).

Agenda-setting is still receiving considerable attention from mass communication theorists who maintain that it is important to understand how the media shape people's views of the major issues in society, even though they may not be the dominant ones in reality. Criticisms that have been levelled against agenda-setting include the view of

McQuail (1987), for example, who asserts that agenda-setting is a plausible but unproven idea, rather than a fully developed theory. He argues that research studies have not provided sufficient evidence to confirm a connection between the order of importance placed on issues by the media and the significance attached to those issues by the public.

7.6.2 Spiral of silence theory

A theory that ascribes far more power to the mass media than agenda-setting is the *spiral of silence theory* developed by Noelle-Neumann (1973; 1980). The underlying argument in this theory is that the media **do** have powerful effects, but that these effects have been underestimated or undetected in the past because of the limitations of research. The spiral of silence explains why some opinions are publicly expressed, whereas others are not discussed in public.

The basic assumption of the spiral of silence theory is that the media effectively limit the range of opinions available to the public. Noelle-Neumann argues that because all media tend to concentrate on the same news stories, the public receives a unified picture of an issue from newspapers, magazines, television and radio stations. This unified picture creates the impression that most people view a controversial issue in the same way as the media. By paying attention to the media, people obtain an idea — often a distorted one — of the distribution of opinion in society. If people find that their own opinion on a particular issue coincides with the majority opinion expressed in media messages, they will be more likely to express and act on this opinion. If, on the other hand, their opinion is not supported by the messages disseminated by the media, they are more likely to keep quiet about it, to refrain from action, and thus to be caught up in the spiral of silence. The more they remain silent, the more other people feel that the particular point of view is not represented, and the more they too remain silent. In political elections, for example, people are sensitive to the prevailing opinion about candidates and issues, and they are more likely to express their preferences when they know these are shared by others. The spiral of silence is not just a matter of wanting to be on 'the winning side', but is an attempt to avoid being isolated from one's social group. The mass media affect the spiral of silence by shaping impressions about which opinions are dominant, and which opinions people can utter in public without becoming isolated. At the same time, they effectively silence the discussion of others. Noelle-Neumann believes that this influence is especially powerful today because of the pervasiveness and repetitiveness of media messages (Noelle-Neumann 1973; Severin & Tankard 1988; Littlejohn 1992; Hunt & Ruben 1993).

According to Littlejohn (1992), the spiral of silence exemplifies careful theory building through research. Beginning with an assumption (that the media effectively limit the range of opinions available to the public), Noelle-Neumann conducted numerous studies over a period of years to test the basic assumption and its ramifications. At the same time, however, the theory does not seem to apply in all societies. A study of public opinion in the Philippine revolution, for example, showed that no spiral of silence appeared to limit alternative views which were publicly expressed, or to favour the dominant opinion in society.

7.7   Audiences of mass communication

Some of the research into the effects of mass communication has been directed at investigating the nature of the mass audience. Prior to the 1930s, theorists assumed that individual members within the audience were passive receivers of mass media messages. Media messages were therefore capable of directly influencing the values, opinions and emotions of the audience. They took it for granted that individual audience members share the same psychological and emotional characteristics. It was also assumed that individual recipients of mass communication lived in isolation and did not interact with others. Media messages would therefore have a predictable and uniform effect on all the members. This argument of uniform and powerful direct media effects was labelled the ***magic bullet***

magic bullet

or *hypodermic-needle theory*, and later became known as the *stimulus-response theory*. Messages had only to be loaded, directed at the target, and fired; if they hit their target, then the expected response would be forthcoming. For example, the results of early research studies showed that people could easily be manipulated by advertising and political propaganda messages communicated by the mass media (Heath & Bryant 1992). After additional investigation, mass communication theorists concluded that the earlier research results could not be substantiated, and several alternative theories about the influence of the media were put forward.

During the 1940s researchers concluded that, while the mass media do have a profound effect on the audience, several other intervening factors modify the uniform response to messages. Studies at that time showed that recipients of mass messages are not isolated individuals, but that they interact with others — family members, friends and work colleagues — who influence their opinions on a variety of matters, such as their voting behaviour. Several people who were interviewed during the study revealed that they obtained most of their information from **other people** (who had received it directly from the mass media) before they learned about it on the media. Drawing on these findings, Katz and Lazarsfeld (1955) developed the two-step flow theory of mass communication.

7.7.1 Two-step flow theory

The two-step flow theory asserts that information from the media moves or flows in two stages. Firstly, certain people who are heavy or regular users of the mass media receive the information. These people, called **opinion leaders**, then pass the information along to others, who are less exposed to the media, through informal, interpersonal communication. Opinion leaders, in retransmitting the information, tend to include their own interpretation of the information in addition to the actual media content, thereby modifying the influence of the mass media. The two-step flow theory is illustrated by the model in figure 7.2.

opinion leaders

Figure 7.2: Two-step flow model of media influence compared with the traditional model of mass communication

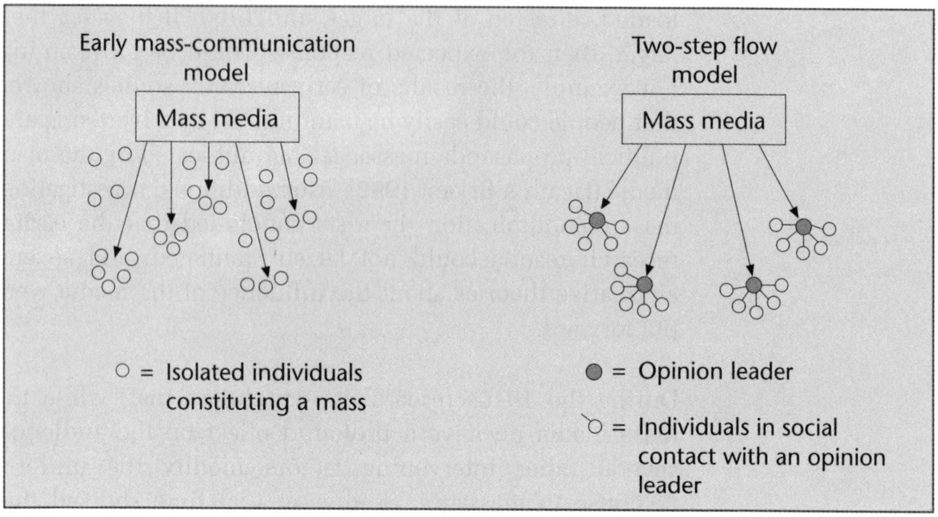

Early mass-communication model

Mass media

Two-step flow model

Mass media

○ = Isolated individuals constituting a mass

● = Opinion leader

○ = Individuals in social contact with an opinion leader

(Adapted by McQuail & Windahl 1981 from Katz & Lazarsfeld 1955)

Several characteristics of opinion leaders have been identified. For instance, they are not always prominent people in the community, but are found at all levels of society. Opinion leaders often have similar beliefs to those they influence. They are reasonably successful in persuading people to change their attitudes and behaviours because they are perceived as being experts in their field. In addition, because the exchange of information takes place in an interpersonal situation, the opinion leader is able to respond to questions and discuss the matter; something that the mass media are unable to do (Infante, Rancer & Womack 1990; Heath & Bryant 1992).

The two-step flow theory of mass communication has helped to **predict** the influence of media messages on audiences and to **explain** why certain media campaigns fail to alter audience attitudes and beliefs. It has also been criticised on the grounds that many major news stories are first heard on the media, and are then discussed interpersonally. The assassination of public figures like John F Kennedy and Chris Hani are events which most people first learned about from the mass media and then discussed among themselves. Also, the implication that opinion leaders are active recipients, and that followers are passive consumers of information, has been found to be too simplistic and not entirely true. Nevertheless, the concept of two-step flow was instrumental in guiding future research which would lead to more complex theories about the influence of mass communication and the idea that mass audiences are active recipients of information.

7.7.2 Uses and gratifications theory

Largely in reaction to the growing dissatisfaction about the direct effects of mass communication on passive audiences, a number of recent mass media theorists have argued that the most important factors governing the effects of mass communication are the needs and interests of audience members. They have focused their attention not on what the media **do to** people, but on what people **do with** the media. Think back for a moment to our criticism of functionalism. The four functions described by Lasswell (1948) and Wright (1960) represent functions of the **content** (messages) of the mass media and neglect to take into account the way audiences **use** that content for their own purposes. In other words, for what functions are mass media messages used by audience members? An analysis of how an audience member actively uses the media is explained by uses and gratifications theory.

Uses and gratifications theory suggests that basic human needs motivate individuals to attend to particular mass media, and to select and use media messages in ways they find personally gratifying. Thus, a given medium, such as radio, and a certain set of messages, such as weather information, might be used by different individuals in very different ways, depending on the particular needs and interests they are seeking to satisfy. On the other hand, some audience members may have no use for this information at all (Hunt & Ruben 1993).

Perhaps the best way to understand uses and gratifications is to think about the process suggested by the theory. Acting on the basis that you have a need to satisfy, for instance the need to relax after a hard day of study, you consider all the options provided by the mass media. From these options, you choose firstly the medium you think will best satisfy that need and secondly a particular item or programme offered by that medium. You may decide between doing the crossword puzzle in the newspaper, listening to a talk show on radio, or watching a soap opera on television. Your individual characteristics, needs and interests will largely determine the choice you make. The degree of gratification (or nongratification) that results from your choice will influence decisions you make in the future.

One of the results of uses and gratifications research has been the identification of basic need categories that can be satisfied through media choices. Heath and Bryant (1992) suggest five categories which show that mass communication can satisfy many of the needs we discussed in unit 3 with reference to interpersonal communication.

▶ **Cognitive needs.** Needs related to acquiring information, knowledge and understanding of our environment, as well as satisfying our curiosity.

▶ **Affective needs.** Needs related to the pursuit of pleasure and entertainment and the satisfaction of our emotions.

▶ **Personal integrative needs.** Needs related to the individual's desire for self-esteem and self-actualisation.

▶ **Social integrative needs.** Needs related to strengthening contact with family, friends and the world.

▶ **Escapist needs.** Needs related to escape, tension release, and the desire for diversion (Heath & Bryant 1992).

Uses and gratifications research has a practical application in that it helps mass media organisations to determine the motivations of their audiences and to serve them more efficiently. It has, however, been criticised for being vague in defining and explaining the concept of *needs* and for producing inaccurate results. It has been suggested that respondents in research studies **infer** the needs they seek to satisfy from questions that are asked about why they use the media, leading to the suspicion that the need was created by the media. Like functionalism, to which it is related, uses and gratifications has also been criticised for being a conservative approach that looks primarily at the positive ways in which individuals meet their needs, without any attention to the possible negative effects of media in society. Nevertheless, it provides a refreshing change from the traditional viewpoint of the passive, unthinking audience (Severin & Tankard 1988; Littlejohn 1992).

Case 7.1

Let us assume that you open your favourite newspaper or magazine and read the advertisement reproduced on the following page. It attracts your interest and you spend some time studying the picture and reading the information. The next thing you know is that your are daydreaming about how wonderful it would be to go on holiday to an exotic destination like Mauritius — a place you have often heard about, but never visited. The fact that you have never been out of South Africa, or even travelled within South Africa by air, makes the idea of such a holiday even more appealing.

After studying the advertisement on page 200, answer the following questions.

1   Who are the communicators?

2   What product or service is being advertised?

3   What are the demographic and psychographic characteristics of the audience at which the advertisement is aimed?

4   Which needs and gratifications are addressed in the advertisement? Explain your answer.

5   Do the nonverbal cues in the picture (for example the human-like figure, the bird) contribute to the verbal message? Explain your answer.

IN AFRICA, WE TOOK THE ART OF TRAVEL AND GAVE IT WINGS.

In an ancient world, man looked up and spread his arms and dreamed of flying. It is a dream as old as the stones and dust of the earth.

We of Africa took this dream and turned it into a work of art. In this vast and endless land we learned more about the magic of travel than anybody else.

We know how to take the traveller into worlds unknown…worlds of luxury, comfort and warmth. And in our quest to create an exceptional experience in flying we have been rewarded in a special way by the readers of Britain's *Executive Travel* magazine. For five consecutive years they have voted South African Airways their airline of choice to Africa.. But for us the quest does not end there; we are moving the dream of travel beyond the ordinary. We have given it wings.

SOUTH AFRICAN AIRWAYS

A Division of Transnet Limited

LINDSAY SMITHERS-FCB 7412

Reproduced with the kind permission of Lindsay-Smithers.

Summary

In this unit we have tried to reach an understanding of some aspects of mass communication. We began by going back in time and looking at five stages in the history of human communication: the age of speech and language; the age of writing; the age of print; the age of the electronic mass media; and the information age. We then continued with a discussion of modern mass communication. We first explained the terms *mass*, *mass communication* and *mass media*. The distinction between mass communication and mass media is important to our understanding of the mass communication context. The process of mass communication was discussed by contrasting it with interpersonal communication and then illustrating the process by means of a model. The next topic we discussed was the functions that mass communication performs in society. In the remainder of the unit we broadened our understanding of mass communication and its influence on society and people by examining the components of the mass communication process in greater detail: the mass communicator, the mass medium and the audiences of mass communication. We referred to various research studies and theories that attempt to explain the effects of mass media messages on society and on people: gatekeeping, agenda-setting, spiral of silence, magic-bullet, two-step flow and uses and gratification theory. The unit ended with a case study based on an advertisement for South African Airways.

Test-yourself

1   Five major stages of the development of human communication are distinguished according to different 'ages'.

   (a)   List each age in historical order.

   (b)   Write down the medium or technological development that characterised each age.

   (c)   Briefly describe the most important social outcome(s) of each new development.

2 Contrast mass communication with interpersonal communication by describing five differences between them.

3 Briefly describe the effects of the mass media on public opinion according to:

   (a) the agenda-setting theory

   (b) the spiral of silence theory

4 Briefly describe how the mass media influences its audience, according to:

   (a) the magic-bullet theory

   (b) the two-step flow theory

   (c) the uses and gratifications theory

Suggested reading

Baal, MB. 1983. *Exploration of agenda-setting in the news magazine '60 minutes'.* MA dissertation. Arizona: University of Arizona.

Clarke, AC. 1945. Extra-terrestrial relays: can rocket stations give world-wide coverage? *Wireless World* (October):305–308.

Crowley, D & Heyer, P. 1991. *Communication in history: technology, culture, society.* New York: Longman.

DeFleur, D. 1994. *Understanding mass communication.* 5th edition. Boston: Houghton Mifflin.

Fang, I. 1997. *A history of mass communication: six information revolutions.* Boston: Focal Press.

Gunter, B & Wober, M. 1991. *The reactive viewer: a review of research on audience reaction measurement.* London: J Libbey.

McQuail, D. 1987. *Mass communication theory: an introduction.* Beverly Hills, CA: Sage

Pei, M. 1965. *The story of language.* Philadelphia: Lippincott.

Rosengren, KE, Wenner, LA & Palmgreen, P. 1985. *Media gratifications research: current perspectives.* Beverly Hills, Calif: Sage.

Schramm, W. 1988. *The story of human communication: cave painting to microchip.* New York: Harper & Row.

Severin, WJ & Tankard, JW. 1992. *Communication theories: origins, methods, uses.* 3rd edition. New York: Longman.

Sources

Abrams, KS. 1986. *Communication at work*. Englewood Cliffs, NJ: Prentice-Hall.

Adelstein, ME & Sparrow, WK. 1990. *Business communications*. 2nd edition. Orlando, Fl: Harcourt, Brace, Javanovich.

Agee, WK, Ault, PH & Emery, E. 1988. *Introduction to mass communication*. 9th edition. New York: Harper & Row.

Alberti, RE & Emmons, ML. 1986. *Your perfect right: a guide to assertive living*. 5th edition. California: Impact.

Allport, GW. 1958. *The nature of prejudice*. Garden City, NY: Doubleday.

Andrews, PH & Baird, JE. 1992. *Communication for business and the professions*. 5th edition. Dubuque, Iowa: Wm C Brown.

Anstey, M. 1991. *Negotiating conflict — insights and skills for negotiators and peacemakers*. Cape Town: Juta.

Applbaum, RL, Bodaken, EM, Sereno, KK & Anatol, KWE. 1979. *The process of group communication*. Chicago: Science Research Associates.

Arnold, W & Libby, R. 1970. *The semantics of sex-related terms* (paper delivered at the annual convention of the Speech Communication Association, Chicago, December 1970).

Aronson, E. 1980. *The social animal*. San Francisco: Freeman.

Asante, MK & Asante, KW (eds). 1990. *African culture: the rhythms of unity*. Trenton, NY: First Africa World Press.

Barker, LL. 1984. *Communication*. 3rd edition. Englewood Cliffs, NJ: Prentice-Hall.

Barker, LL & Gaut, DA. 1996. *Communication*. Boston: Allyn & Bacon.

Barnlund, DC. 1970. A transactional model of communication, in *Foundations of communication theory*, edited by KK Sereno & CD Mortensen. New York: Harper & Row.

Bavelas, A. 1950. Communication patterns in task-oriented groups. *Journal of Acoustical Society of America* (22):725–730.

Beal, MB. 1983. *Exploration of agenda-setting in the news magazine '60 minutes'.* MA dissertation. Arizona: University of Arizona.

Benjamin, JB. 1986. *Communication: concepts and contexts.* New York: Harper & Row.

Benne, KD & Sheats, P. 1948. Functional roles of group members. *Journal of Social Issues* (4): 41–49.

Berko, RM, Wolvin, AD & Curtis, R. 1986. *This business of communicating.* 3rd edition. Dubuque, Iowa: Wm C Brown.

Bersheid, E. 1985. Interpersonal attraction, in *Handbook of Social Psychology,* edited by G Lindzey & E Aronson. New York: Random House.

Bettinghaus, EP. 1968. *Persuasive communication.* New York: Holt, Rinehart & Winston.

Birdwhistell, RL. 1970. *Kinesics and context: essays on body motion communication.* Philadelphia: University of Pennsylvania Press.

Bittner, JR. 1985. *Fundamentals of communication.* Englewood Cliffs, NJ: Prentice-Hall.

Blumberg, RL. 1987. *Organizations in contemporary society.* Englewood Cliffs, NJ: Prentice-Hall.

Bormann, EG & Bormann, NC. 1988. *Effective small group communication.* 4th edition. Minneapolis: Burgess International Group.

Botha, H. 1997. The history and development of film and television, in *Introduction to communication: course book 6 – film and television studies,* edited by PJ Fourie. Cape Town: Juta.

Bowra, CM. 1966. *Classical Greece.* Nederland NV: Time-Life.

Bredenkamp, C. 1996. Persuasive communication, in *Introduction to communication: course book 4 – communication planning and management,* edited by R Rensburg. Cape Town: Juta.

Briggs, K. 1986. Assertiveness: speak your mind. *Nursing Times* (82): 24–26.

Brilhart, JK. 1989. *Effective group discussion.* 6th edition. Dubuque, Iowa: Wm C Brown.

Brown, R. 1986. *Social psychology.* 2nd edition. New York: Free Press.

Brownell, J. 1986. *Building active listening skills.* Englewood Cliffs, NJ: Prentice-Hall.

Buber, M. 1964. *Between man and man.* London: Collins.

Buber, M. 1970. *I and thou.* Edinburgh: Clark.

Burgoon, JK, Boller, BB & Woodall, WG. 1989. *Nonverbal communication: the unspoken dialogue.* New York: Harper & Row.

Burley-Allen, M. 1982. *Listening: the forgotten skill.* New York: Wiley.

Burton, G & Dimbleby, R. 1995. *Between ourselves.* 2nd edition. London: Edward Arnold.

Carbaugh, D (ed). 1990. *Cultural communication and intercultural contact.* Hillsdale, NJ: Lawrence Erlbaum.

Clarke, AC. 1945. Extra-terrestrial relays: can rocket stations give world-wide coverage? *Wireless World* (October):305–308.

Cook, M. 1971. *Interpersonal perception.* Baltimore: Penguin.

Corman, SR, Banks, SP, Bantz, CR & Mayer, ME (eds). 1990. *Foundations of organizational communication: a reader.* New York: Longman.

Crowley, D & Heyer, P. 1991. *Communication in history: technology, culture, society.* New York: Longman.

Dahnke, GL & Clatterbuck, GW (eds). 1990. *Human communication: theory and research.* Belmont, Calif: Wadsworth.

Dance, FEX. 1970. The 'concept' of communication. *Journal of Communication* (20):201–210.

Dance, FEX & Larson, CE. 1976. *The functions of human communication: a theoretical approach.* New York: Holt, Rinehart & Winston.

Daniels, TD & Spiker, BK. 1987. *Perspectives on organizational communication.* Dubuque, Iowa: Wm C Brown.

De Beer, AS (ed). 1993. *Mass media for the nineties: the South African handbook of mass communication.* Johannesburg: Van Schaik.

Deetz, SA (ed). 1993. *Communication yearbook 16.* Newbury Park: Sage.

DeFleur, D. 1994. *Understanding mass communication.* 5th edition. Boston: Houghton Mifflin.

De Fleur, ML & Ball-Rokeach, SJ. 1989. *Theories of mass communication.* 5th edition. New York: Longman.

Delia, JG. 1980. Some tentative thoughts concerning the study of interpersonal relationships and their development. *Western Journal of Speech Communication* (44): 97–107.

DeVito, JA. 1986. *The communication handbook.* New York: Harper & Row.

DeVito, JA. 1989. *The interpersonal communication book.* New York: Harper & Row.

DeVito, JA. 1990. *Messages: building interpersonal communication skills.* New York: Harper & Row.

DeVito, JA & Hecht, ML (eds). 1990. *The nonverbal communication reader.* Prospect Heights, Ill: Waveland.

De Wet, JC. 1991. *The art of persuasive communication.* Cape Town: Juta.

Dickson, DA, Hargie, O & Morrow, NC. 1989. *Communication skills training for health professionals: an instructor's handbook.* London: Chapman & Hall.

Dimbleby, R & Burton, G. 1985. *More than words: an introduction to communication.* London: Routledge.

Dimbleby, R & Burton, G. 1992. *More than words: an introduction to communication.* 2nd edition. London: Routledge.

Druckman, D. 1982. *Nonverbal communication: survey, theory and research.* Beverly Hills, Calif: Sage.

Du Plooy, GM. 1991. *500 communication concepts.* Cape Town: Juta.

Du Plooy, GM. 1994. *Communication: only study guide for CMN100-Q (Introduction to communication science).* Pretoria: University of South Africa.

Du Plooy, GM. 1995. *Communication: only study guide for CMN212–X (Communication semiotics).* Pretoria: University of South Africa.

Du Plooy, GM. 1996. Nonverbal communication and meaning, in *Introduction to communication: course book 3 — communication and the production of meaning,* edited by PJ Fourie. Cape Town: Juta.

Ekeh, P. 1974. *Social exchange theory.* London: Heinemann.

Ekman, P & Friesen, WV. 1969. The repertoire of nonverbal behaviour: categories, usage and coding. *Semiotica* (1): 49–98.

Ellis, R & McClintock, A. 1994. *If you take my meaning: theory and practice in human communication.* 2nd edition. London: Edward Arnold.

Fabre, M. 1969. *A history of communications.* London: Leisure Arts.

Finlayson, R. 1991. Education in a multicultural environment. *Transvaal Educational News* (August): 6–11.

Fisher, AB. 1980. *Small-group decision making: communication and the group process.* 2nd edition. New York: McGraw-Hill.

Fisher, D. 1981. *Communication in organizations.* New York: West.

Floyd, JJ. 1985. *Listening: a practical approach.* Glenview,Ill: Scott Foresman.

Furnham, A. 1979. Assertiveness in three cultures: multidimensionality and cultural differences. *Journal of Clinical Psychology* (35): 522–527.

Gamble, TK & Gamble, M. 1987. *Communication works.* 2nd edition. New York: Random House.

Gerbner, G & Schramm, W. 1990. The international development of communication studies. *Communicatio* 16(1):8–18.

Gibson, IW & Hanna, NS. 1992. *Introduction to human communication.* Dubuque, Iowa: Wm C Brown.

Glean, EC & Pood, EA. 1989. Listening self-inventory. *Supervisory Management* (34):12–15.

Goffman, E. 1975. *The presentation of self in everyday life.* Garden City, NY: Doubleday.

Goldhaber, GM. 1990. *Organizational communication.* 5th edition. Dubuque, Iowa: Wm C Brown.

Gudykunst, W & Ting-Toomey, S. 1988. *Culture and interpersonal communication.* Newbury Park, Calif: Sage.

Gunter, B & Wober, M. 1991. *The reactive viewer: a review of research on audience reaction measurement.* London: Libbey.

Hall, ET. 1969. *The hidden dimension.* New York: Doubleday.

Hall, ET. 1973. *The silent language.* Garden City, NY: Anchor Books.

Hall, ET & Hall, MR. 1990. *Understanding cultural differences.* Yarmouth, Maine: Intercultural Press.

Hamilton, C & Parker, C. 1990. *Communicating for results.* 3rd edition. Belmont, Calif: Wadsworth.

Hartley, P. 1993. *Interpersonal communication.* London: Routledge.

Heath, RL & Bryant, J. 1992. *Human communication theory and research: concepts, contexts and challenges.* Hillsdale, NJ: Lawrence Erlbaum.

Heun, LR & Heun, RE. 1978. *Developing skills for human interaction.* 2nd edition. Columbus, Ohio: Merrill.

Hickson, ML & Stacks, DW. 1989. *Nonverbal communication: studies and applications.* 2nd edition. Dubuque, Iowa: Wm C Brown.

Homans, GC. 1959. *The human group.* New York: Harcourt, Brace & World.

Homans, GC. 1961. *Social behaviour: its elementary forms.* New York: Harcourt, Brace & World.

Hoover, K. 1979. *The elements of social scientific thinking.* 2nd edition. New York: St Martin's Press.

Hunt, T & Ruben, BD. 1993. *Mass communication producers and consumers.* New York: HarperCollins.

Hybels, S & Weaver, RL. 1995. *Communicating effectively.* 4th edition. New York: Random House.

Infante, DA, Rancer, AS & Womack, DF. 1990. *Building communication theory.* Prospect Heights, Ill: Waveland.

Innes, D, Kentridge, M & Perold, H (eds). 1993. *Reversing discrimination: affirmative action in the workplace.* Cape Town: Oxford University Press.

Janis, I. 1972. Groupthink. *Psychology Today* (5):43–46; 74–76.

Jansen, N. 1989. *Philosophy of mass communication research.* Cape Town: Juta.

Jansen, N & Steinberg, S. 1991. *Theoretical approaches to communication.* Cape Town: Juta.

Johannensen, RL. 1971. The emerging concept of communication as dialogue. *Quarterly Journal of Communication* 62(4):373–382.

Johannensen, RL. 1990. *Ethics in human communication.* 4th edition. Prospect Heights, III: Waveland.

Jouard, S. 1964. *The transparent self.* New York: Van Nostrand Reinhold.

Katz, E & Lazarsfeld, PF. 1955. *Personal influence.* Glencoe: Free Press.

Kleinke, C. 1986. *Meeting and understanding people.* New York: Freeman.

Knapp, ML. 1980. *Essentials of nonverbal communication.* New York: Holt, Rinehart & Winston.

Knapp, ML. 1984. *Interpersonal communication and human relationships.* Newton, Maine: Allyn & Bacon.

Knapp, ML. 1990. Nonverbal communication: basic perspectives, in *Bridges not walls: a book about interpersonal communication*, edited by J Stewart. New York: McGraw-Hill.

Koehler, JW, Anatol, KWE & Applbaum, RL. 1981. *Organizational communication: behavioral perspectives.* New York: Holt, Rinehart & Winston.

Kreps, GL. 1990. *Organizational communication: theory and practice.* 2nd edition. New York: Longman..

Lange, AJ & Jabukowski, P. 1976. *Responsible assertive behaviour.* Champaign, Ill: Research.

Larson, CU. 1989. *Persuasion, reception and responsibility.* 5th edition. Belmont, Calif: Wadsworth.

Lasswell, HD. 1948. The structure and function of communication in society, in *The communication of ideas*, edited by E Bryson. New York: Harper & Brothers.

Leavitt, HJ. 1951. Some effects of certain communication patterns on group performance. *Journal of Abnormal and Social Psychology* (46):38–50.

Liebes, T. 1988. Cultural differences in the retelling of television fiction. *Critical Studies in Mass Communication* (5): 277–292.

Littlejohn, S. 1983. *Theories of human communication.* 2nd edition. Belmont, Calif: Wadsworth.

Littlejohn, S. 1992. *Theories of human communication.* 4th edition. Belmont, Calif: Wadsworth.

Louw, PE. 1993. *South African media policy: debates of the 1990s.* Belville: Anthropos.

Luft, J. 1970. *Of human interaction.* Palo Alto, Calif: National Press.

Lustig, MW & Koester, J. 1993. *Intercultural competence: interpersonal communication across cultures.* New York: HarperCollins.

Malandro, LA, Barker, L & Barker, DA. 1989. *Nonverbal communication.* 2nd edition. New York: Random House.

Martin, LJ & Hiebert, RE (eds). 1990. *Current issues in international communication.* New York: London Press.

Maslow, AH. 1954. *Motivation and personality.* New York: Harper & Row.

McGregor, D. 1960. *The human side of enterprise.* New York: McGraw-Hill.

McLuhan, M. 1973. *Understanding media: the extensions of man.* New York: New American Library.

McQuail, D. 1987. *Mass communication theory: an introduction.* Beverly Hills, Calif: Sage.

McQuail, D & Windahl, S. 1981. *Communication models for the study of mass communications.* New York: Longman.

Mehrabian, A. 1981. *Silent messages.* 2nd edition. Belmont, Calif: Wadsworth.

Myers, MT & Myers, GB. 1982. *Managing by communication: an organisational approach.* New York: McGraw-Hill.

Noelle-Neumann, E. 1973. Return to the concept of powerful mass media, in *Studies of broadcasting: an international annual of broadcasting science,* edited by H Eguchi & K Sata. Tokyo: Nippon Hoso, Kyokai.

Noelle-Neumann, E.1980. Mass media and social change in developed societies, in *Mass communication review yearbook,* vol 1, edited by GC Wilhoit & H de Bock. Beverly Hills, Calif: Sage.

Nutting, J & White, G. 1990. *This business of communicating.* 2nd edition. Roseville. New South Wales: McGraw-Hill.

O'Sullivan, T, Hartley, J, Saunders, D & Fiske, J. 1989. *Key concepts in communication.* London: Routledge.

Pace, RW. 1983. *Organizational communication: foundations for human resource development.* Englewood Cliffs, NJ: Prentice-Hall.

Pavitt, C. 1990. The ideal communicator as the basis for competence of self and friend. *Communication Reports* (3):9–14.

Pearson, J. 1985. *Gender and communication.* Dubuque, Iowa: Wm C Brown.

Pearson, JC & Spitzberg, BH. 1990. *Interpersonal communication: concepts, components and contexts.* 2nd edition. Dubuque, Iowa: Wm C Brown.

Pease, A & Garner, A. 1989. *Talk language: how to use conversation for profit and pleasure.* London: Simon & Schuster.

Pei, M. 1965. *The story of language.* Philadelphia: Lippincott.

Phillips, GM. 1982. *Communicating in organizations.* New York: MacMillan.

Postman, N. 1990. Crazy talk, stupid talk, in *Bridges not walls: a book about interpersonal communication*, edited by J Stewart. New York: McGraw-Hill.

Poyatos, F (ed). 1988. *Cross-cultural perspectives in nonverbal communication.* Toronto, CJ: Hogrefe.

Rakos, R. 1986. Asserting and confronting, in *A handbook of communication skills*, edited by O Hargie. London: Croom Helm.

Redding, C. 1972. *Communication within the organisation.* New York: Industrial Communication Council.

Rensburg, R & Bredenkamp, C. 1991. *Aspects of business communication.* Cape Town: Juta.

Roberts, WR. 1924. *Works of Aristotle.* Oxford: Clarendon Press.

Roethlisberger, FJ & Dickson, WJ. 1939. *Management and the worker.* Cambridge, Mass: Harvard University Press.

Roloff, ME & Miller, GR. 1987. *Interpersonal processes: new directions in communication research.* Beverly Hills, Calif: Sage.

Rosengren, KE, Wenner, LA & Palmgreen, P. 1985. *Media gratifications research: current perspectives.* Beverly Hills, Calif: Sage.

Ruben, BD. 1984. *Communication and human behavior.* New York: MacMillan.

Sagan, C. 1977. *The dragons of Eden: speculations on the evolution of human intelligence.* New York: Ballantine.

Satir, V. 1972. *Peoplemaking.* Palo Alto, Calif: Science and Behavior Books.

Schneider, DJ, Hastorf, AH & Ellsworth, PC. 1979. *Person perception.* Reading, Mass: Addison-Wesley.

Schramm, W. 1965. How communication works, in *The process and effects of mass communication*, edited by W Schramm. Urbana, Ill: University of Illinois Press.

Schramm, W. 1988. *The story of human communication: cave painting to microchip.* New York: Harper & Row.

Schutz, WC. 1958. *The interpersonal underworld.* Reading, Mass: Addison-Wesley.

Severin, WJ & Tankard, JW. 1988. *Communication theories: origins, methods, uses.* 2nd edition. New York: Longman.

Shannon, CE & Weaver, W. 1949. *The mathematical theory of communication.* Urbana: University of Illinois Press.

Shaw, ME. 1981. *Group dynamics: the psychology of small group behavior.* 3rd edition. New York: McGraw-Hill.

Shockley-Zalabak, P. 1991. *Fundamentals of organizational communication: knowledge, sensitivity, skills, values.* New York: Longman.

Shuter, R. 1984. *Communicating.* New York: Holt, Rinehart & Winston.

Stacks, D, Hickson, M & Hill, SR. 1991. *Introduction to communication theory.* Fort Worth: Holt, Rinehart & Winston.

Staley, CC & Staley, RS. 1992. *Communicating in business and the professions: the inside word.* Belmont, Calif: Wadsworth.

Steil, LK, Barker, LL & Watson, KW. 1983. *Effective listening: the key to your success.* Reading, Mass: Addison-Wesley.

Steinberg, S. 1994. *Introduction to communication: course book 1 — the basics.* Cape Town: Juta.

Steinberg, S. 1995. *Communication: only study guide for CMN213–Y (Introduction to communication planning and management).* Pretoria: University of South Africa.

Steinberg, S. 1996. Organisational communication, in *Introduction to communication: course book 4: communication planning and management,* edited by RS Rensburg. Cape Town: Juta.

Stewart, J (ed). 1990. *Bridges not walls: a book about interpersonal communication.* New York: McGraw-Hill.

Strano, Z, Mohan, T & McGregor, H. 1989. *Communicating!* 2nd edition. Sydney: Harcourt Brace Jovanovich.

Terblanche, FH. 1994. Die aard en gemeenskapskulturele dimensie van nieverbale boodskapverkeer met spesifieke verwysing na emblematiese gedrag. *Communitas* (1):32–54.

Trenholm, S.1989. *Persuasion and social influence.* Englewood Cliffs, NJ: Prentice-Hall.

Trenholm, S. 1991. *Human communication theory.* 2nd edition. Englewood Cliffs, NJ: Prentice-Hall.

Tubbs, SL & Moss, S. 1991. *Human communication.* 6th edition. New York: McGraw-Hill.

Van der Merwe, N. 1991. *Listening: a skill for everyone.* Cape Town: Arrow.

Verderber, RF. 1990. *Communicate!* 6th edition. Belmont, Calif: Wadsworth.

Verderber, RF. 1993. *Communicate!* 7th edition. Belmont, Calif: Wadsworth.

Verderber, RF & Verderber, KS. 1992. *Interact: using interpersonal communication skills.* 6th edition. Belmont, Calif: Wadsworth.

Watzlawick, P, Beavin, JH & Jackson, DD. 1968. *Pragmatics of human communication.* New York: Norton.

Wenburg, JR & Wilmot, WW. 1973. *The personal communication process.* New York: John Wiley.

Westrum, R & Samaha, K. 1984. *Complex organizations: growth, struggle and change.* Englewood Cliffs, NJ: Prentice-Hall.

Whetten, DA & Cameron, KS. 1993. *Developing management skills: communicating supportively.* New York: HarperCollins.

White, R & Lippit, R.1960. *Autocracy and democracy: an experimental inquiry.* New York: Harper & Row.

Wilmont,W.1975. *Dyadic communication.* Reading, Mass: Addison-Wesley.

Wilson, GL, Hantz, AM & Hanna, MS. 1989. *Interpersonal growth through communication.* 2nd edition. Dubuque, Iowa: Wm C Brown.

Wolff, FI, Marsnik, NC, Tacey, WS & Nichols, RG. 1983. *Perceptive listening.* New York: Holt, Rinehart & Winston.

Wolvin, AD & Coakley, CG. 1982. *Listening.* Dubuque, Iowa: Wm C Brown.

Wright, CR. 1960. Functional analysis and mass communication. *Public Opinion Quarterly* (24): 605–620.

Zannes, E. 1982. *The widening circle.* Reading, Mass: Addison-Wesley.

Zimbardo, PG & Radl, SL. 1979. *The shyness workbook.* New York: The A&W Visual Library.

Index

internal noises 19
internet 181
interpersonal communication 37
interpretation of meaning 18, 33, 73
intimate distance 55
intrapersonal communication 36–37, 69, 82–83
intrapersonal variations 81–82
I-you relationship 96–97, 100

J
Johari window 87–88

K
kinesics 49–50
knowledge 116

L
laissez-faire leaders 138
language system 169–170
Lasswell's model 27–28, 29, 30, 31, 186, 197
lateral communication 161–162
leadership 135–140
leakage 47
legal restrictions 191
linear process 20–21
listening 99–107

M
magic bullet 194–195
maintenance roles 134
Marconi, inventor 177
Maslow's hierarchy of needs 83, 84–85, 91, 107
mass communication 39, 182–189
mass communicator 183, 189–191
mass, concept of 181–182
mass media 182, 184, 191
mass messages 183
mass recipient 183
meaning 17–18, 188
meaning-centred definition 4–5
media attention 192–193
mediated 183
medieval (Middle Ages) 25

medium 16–17
message 13
Middle Ages (Medieval) 25
models 21–36
mode of existence 96, 98–99
monologue 96
Müller-Lyer illusion 71

N
needs 82–85
news-sheet 175–176
new values (newsworthiness) 190
noise 18–19
nonassertive style 112–113
nonverbal behaviour 117–118
nonverbal communication 6, 7, 43–45
nonverbal signs 13
norms 133
note-taking 106

O
open pane 87
opinion leaders 195
opinions 82
oral communication 7
oratory 23
organisation 73
organisational chart 160
organisational communication 38, 154
    classical approach 155
    human relations approach 156
    human resources approach 157
    systems approach 175–158
overpersonal 108
oversocial 108

P
papyrus-making process 174
paralanguage 59–60
parchment 174
passive style 112
perception of others 70–71, 77–81
perceptual disclosure 73
perceptual inaccuricies 77–79
personal people 109
personal distance 55